The Whole Ninth Floor

A COMEDY

by

Richard Seff

NEW YORK HOLLYWOOD LONDON TORONTO

SAMUELFRENCH.COM

Copyright © 2008 by Richard Seff

ALL RIGHTS RESERVED

CAUTION: Professionals and amateurs are hereby warned that *THE WHOLE NINTH FLOOR* is subject to a royalty. It is fully protected under the copyright laws of the United States of America, the British Commonwealth, including Canada, and all other countries of the Copyright Union. All rights, including professional, amateur, motion picture, recitation, lecturing, public reading, radio broadcasting, television and the rights of translation into foreign languages are strictly reserved. In its present form the play is dedicated to the reading public only.

The amateur live stage performance rights to *THE WHOLE NINTH FLOOR* are controlled exclusively by Samuel French, Inc., and royalty arrangements and licenses must be secured well in advance of presentation. PLEASE NOTE that amateur royalty fees are set upon application in accordance with your producing circumstances. When applying for a royalty quotation and license please give us the number of performances intended, dates of production, your seating capacity and admission fee. Royalties are payable one week before the opening performance of the play to Samuel French, Inc., at 45 W. 25th Street, New York, NY 10010.

Royalty of the required amount must be paid whether the play is presented for charity or gain and whether or not admission is charged.

Stock royalty quoted upon application to Samuel French, Inc.

For all other rights than those stipulated above, apply to Samuel French, Inc., at 45 W. 25th Street, New York, NY 10010.

Particular emphasis is laid on the question of amateur or professional readings, permission and terms for which must be secured in writing from Samuel French, Inc.

Copying from this book in whole or in part is strictly forbidden by law, and the right of performance is not transferable.

Whenever the play is produced the following notice must appear on all programs, printing and advertising for the play: "Produced by special arrangement with Samuel French, Inc."

Due authorship credit must be given on all programs, printing and advertising for the play.

ISBN 978-0-573-66396-3   Printed in U.S.A.   #25761

No one shall commit or authorize any act or omission by which the copyright of, or the right to copyright, this play may be impaired.

No one shall make any changes in this play for the purpose of production.

Publication of this play does not imply availability for performance. Both amateurs and professionals considering a production are strongly advised in their own interests to apply to Samuel French, Inc., for written permission before starting rehearsals, advertising, or booking a theatre.

No part of this book may be reproduced, stored in a retrieval system, or transmitted in any form, by any means, now known or yet to be invented, including mechanical, electronic, photocopying, recording, videotaping, or otherwise, without the prior written permission of the publisher.

IMPORTANT BILLING AND CREDIT REQUIREMENTS

All producers of *THE WHOLE NINTH FLOOR* must give credit to the Author of the Play in all programs distributed in connection with performances of the Play, and in all instances in which the title of the Play appears for the purposes of advertising, publicizing or otherwise exploiting the Play and/or a production. The name of the Author *must* appear on a separate line on which no other name appears, immediately following the title and *must* appear in size of type not less than fifty percent of the size of the title type.

Prior to the publication, ***THE WHOLE NINTH FLOOR*** was staged only once in a 1966 limited run stock production in Paramus, New Jersey. It starred Alan Alda as 'George', featured Grayson Hall as 'Carol', and Evelyn Russell as 'Mildred'. It has been revised, edited and reshaped.

CHARACTERS

(In Order of Appearance)

MILDRED HEINDORPH - In her forties and no beauty.

GLORIA WEST - Young and curvy

ELLEN WOLSKY - Twenty-six, simple, straightforward. She's not really a girl of the 1960s. Her values go back to a quieter time.

LANCE PACKARD - A young twenty-five. Avid, zealous, apt and rich.

HENRY OLDSCHAN - Attractive, in his late twenties. Less volatile than Lance, if he has any neuroses, they don't show.

GEORGE WILSON - Thirty-one, pleasant looking. No one pulls him, no one pushes; he knows where he's going, but not quite how to get there.

CARL MURRAY - Early fifties. Pale, tired, but still trying to stay on the treadmill.

ALEC BRUIN - Thirty, attractive, and superficially charming. Underneath there is an ambitious boy who knows he's not terribly talented and charm will have to go a long way.

MARIA CUEVA - A Mexican beauty. Early twenties, volatile, emotional. Her acting, in English, is early De Mille. A very small role.

FELIX FOWLER - Forty-five and looks younger. Quiet, charming but capable of sudden unexpected bursts of anger.

CAROL BEAUMONT - Between forty and forty-five, it's hard to tell. She's vivid and as refreshing as an autumn breeze in August. A Movie Star.

Suggested Production Note: If the group performing the play needs to have only one intermission, the play can be restructured in the following manner: The first act would end in what is now Act II (on page 57 of this script), and the scene that ends it would now be called Act I - Scene 3. It would require only the following additional lines to accommodate.

MILDRED. Oh my God!

(She hangs up. She crosses at once to Ellen's desk, and in one quick movement, covers Ellen's typewriter even as **ELLEN** *types).*

Get in there, turn off that record and send Gloria back out here. He's on his way down.

ELLEN. Who's on his way down?

MILDRED. Our leader, Felix the First. We've got two minutes!

ELLEN. Mildred, I was writing a letter. That was rude.

MILDRED. If you don't get in there, NOW, close the bar and shut down the disco, there will be no more letters. Understand? There will be un- em – ployment.

ELLEN. You're joking.

MILDRED. This man does not have a sense of humor. None. Now go, girl – go!

ELLEN. Poor George.

MILDRED. Never mind George. It's the whole damned floor he's after!

*(***ELLEN*** runs to George's office.* **MILDRED** *returns to her own desk to straighten up)*

Who needs this? My mother was right. I should have been a nun.

(CURTAIN)

The new second act begins with Act II-Scene 1. Here's how:

ACT II - Scene 1

SETTING: The same

TIME: Immediately following.

AT RISE: **(ELLEN** *bursts into George's office, pulls* **GLORIA** *out of his arms, somewhat against Gloria's wishes)*

Then, continue with the text as is. Act III Scene 1 becomes Act II Scene 2, Act III Scene 2 becomes Act II Scene 3. And there you are, you have a Two Act play. If possible, play it in 3 acts, for it was conceived that way. It should run about two hours and fifteen minutes, even with two intermissions.

A NOTE ABOUT COSTUMES

Just keep in mind the play is set in 1962. For the men: dark suits and thin, conservative ties, with white shirts. One khaki (tan) suit for George Wilson, with red tie in Act III. One bright yellow tie for Henry Oldschan in Act III. The women wear appropriate office wardrobe in the style of the Kennedy years. If you can get a copy of "Mad Men," the AMC Television series, that is the look of this play, set across the street on Madison Avenue in New York at an international talent agency.

DEDICATED TO ALL THOSE WHO LOVE
AND SUPPORT LIVE TEATRE,
BOTH BACKSTAGE
AND FRONT OF HOUSE.

ACT I

Scene 1

*(**THE SCENE:** A section of the ninth floor of the National Talent Agency on Madison Avenue in New York. The stage is divided into two playing areas: stage right is the Secretarial Pool and includes three desks, one each for Ellen Wolsky, Mildred Heindorph and Gloria West. Entrance to this area is from downstage right. At extreme right is a closet. There are two doors Upstage, one leading into Lance Packard's office, the other into Henry Oldschan's. In upstage of the stage left wall of this area, there is a door leading into George Wilson's office. We can move through this door and into Wilson's office, which comprises the stage left area of the set. The office is furnished tastefully, but impersonally, in the finest Old English. Prints on the wall, not oils. It's the kind of "perfect room" that in no way reflects the personality of the man who occupies it, and as that is what the decorator had in mind, it succeeds. Wilson's desk [antique] faces downstage, and there is a large window behind it. On the desk there is a large, leafy plant [artificial]. At extreme stage left, there is a door, leading into a small washroom.)*

*(**AT RISE**: Lights up on Secretarial Pool, down on Wilson's office. At rise, **GLORIA WEST**, young and curvy, is reading an astrology book. **MILDRED HEINDORPH**, who is forty and no beauty, has a phone to her ear, waiting impatiently.)*

*(**TIME:** Ten-thirty. Monday morning: early September, 1962.)*

MILDRED. *(on phone)* Mrs. Miller, I am waiting!

(Then, to **GLORIA:***)*

I could turn blue for all she'd care.

GLORIA. She's probably got you on 'hold.' They do that.

(Her phone rings.)

Mr. Oldschan's office. Yes, this is the theatre department – Madame, you – four languages and the bugle, too? Mm. Mm. And tap dances? – Madame – Madame – I'm sorry, you'll have to send in a picture and resumé.

(hangs up)

MILDRED. A stage mother, right?

GLORIA. With an eight year old named Sandra.

MILDRED. *(into phone:)* Oh, there you are, Mrs. Miller. Now, where the hell is our coffee? – well, he'd better have just left!

(hangs up)

GLORIA. *(She's reading her book again.)* Did you have a late night?

MILDRED. They showed "Citizen Kane" on the tube and it's eight hours long.

GLORIA. Oh, look – it's good things today for Libra. That's me! I'm Libra.

MILDRED. Well, I'm Cancer. The Crab?

GLORIA. Cancer?

(looks in book)

Uh oh. It's not a good time for you romantically.

MILDRED. I needed you to tell me, right?

*(***ELLEN WOLSKY** *enters, carrying coffee in a paper bag.)*

ELLEN. Good morning, girls. I brought your coffee.

MILDRED. Thank God. Really, I've started to shake.

GLORIA. Yes, you have. And you're mean.

ELLEN. *(hands it out)* I met the boy in the elevator.

MILDRED. You're a doll. And don't you look Doris Daysie.

ELLEN. *(fluffing her hair)* You like it? Hairdresser before breakfast.

MILDRED. On a Monday?

ELLEN. I went fishing all weekend, my hair needed doing, and I had it done. Period.

MILDRED. I never said a word.

ELLEN. Well, don't. And I baked us some cookies.

GLORIA. Not me, honey. This is think thin week.

ELLEN. I'll put them in the closet.

(She does so. ELLEN's phone rings.)

MILDRED. Ah, ha! Some rotten little client wakes up, grunts, and wants his agent.

ELLEN. Oh, you.

(picks up phone)

Mr. Wilson's office. No, Martha – he's due back from Ohio this morning – Martha, wait!

(hands over phone)

My God, it's Mr. Fowler!

GLORIA. *(rising)* Mr. Fowler!? Himself?!

MILDRED. You don't have to rise, dear. He's only President here. Mr. Kennedy's still in the White House.

GLORIA. I've never met him. I've only SEEN him once.

ELLEN. Shhh!

(then, into phone:)

Yes, Martha, I'm still here. Yes, Martha, I'll give him the message.

(hangs up)

Oh dear, Fowler wants to see George at eleven.

GLORIA. Ooooh. Our president. What's he doing in town? Does he ever come down to visit?

MILDRED. Once in a while he inspects everybody's drawers. He's a neatness nut.

GLORIA. I've got "Peyton Place" in my drawer.

MILDRED. If he does have a raid, I'll be tipped off in advance.

ELLEN. Fowler comes to New York for one day and wants to see George. Why? Poor George.

MILDRED. Poor George. I thought you washed your hair for Gloria and me.

ELLEN. You know, Gloria's right. You are mean.

(**LANCE PACKARD** *enters. Twenty-five, eager, boyish and likeable. Today, He is slightly manic.*)

LANCE. Mildred, I'd like to see you in my office. Now!

(*He disappears into his office, and slams the door.*)

MILDRED. It's one laugh after another.

(*As she moves into* **LANCE**'s *office, to* **ELLEN.**)

Don't lose your place. I'm not mean. I'm honest, and I want to talk to you.

ELLEN. I'll be here.

GLORIA. We think you're wasting your time. Bosses don't marry their secretaries.

ELLEN. So?

GLORIA. So – we hate your spending your weekend fishing when you should be out in the market place looking over the merchandise.

ELLEN. I can't do that.

GLORIA. And every time George Wilson says "come on, kid, I'll buy you a hamburger," you grab your purse and run. It's just wrong.

ELLEN. You've been talking to my mother.

GLORIA. I have not. It's your life. If you want to play 'brother and sister', it's fine with me.

(*Her buzzer rings twice.*)

My Lord and Master. Remind me, no more bosses who get in early.

(*As she gathers steno pads, etc., and reaches Henry's*

door.)

And remember you heard it from Gloria first. Neptune's been falling in your chart. You are headed for trouble.

(She exits, **MILDRED** *re-enters.)*

MILDRED. He's discovered an actress from Mexico. He wants me to teach him Spanish. By lunchtime.

ELLEN. Can you do that?

MILDRED. I can get him through lunch. But don't change the subject. I'm not mean. I care about you and...

(Now, **GEORGE WILSON** *enters, carrying two suitcases.)*

GEORGE. Hello! And look who's here. Mildred, you old gargoyle!

MILDRED. I'm going to say a nice thing. I missed you, George.

GEORGE. Of course you did.

MILDRED. Didn't you miss me?

GEORGE. Too busy, watching a star being born.

MILDRED. Tell me!

(Her intercom buzzes.)

Later.

(into phone:)

Hello.

ELLEN. Oh George, it's so good to see you. A whole week.

GEORGE. Come on in.

ELLEN. I'll get the mail.

GEORGE. But slowly, I'm still on Ohio tempo.

MILDRED. *(hangs up her phone)* Do you KNOW what Berlitz charges for Spanish?

(moves toward **LANCE**'s *door)*

It's a good thing I'm fully vested in the Profit Sharing Plan, because I am terribly valuable to this company!

*(She goes into **LANCE**'s office.)*

ELLEN. *(to **GEORGE**)* Did you bring coffee?

GEORGE. Shhh. It's in my briefcase.

ELLEN. I'll get a cup. You go in and get settled.

GEORGE. How did it go? Any major disasters?

ELLEN. Oh – uh – how was your flight?

*(**ELLEN** gets cup and saucer from her closet; **GEORGE** moves into his office, puts away the suitcases in the little room off left, and removes coffee from his briefcase. **ELLEN** joins him in his office, and during the next scene pours his coffee. The lights fade on Secretarial Pool area.)*

GEORGE. The flight was fine – I was terrible. The seatbelt came off in my hand, and I swear the plane was leaking all through Pennsylvania.

*(**ELLEN** gives him his cup, the mail, and the phone message sheet.)*

ELLEN. Here's the mail, and a list of phone messages.

GEORGE. Not yet. I tell you Janet Babcock was worth the whole trek. Six months ago her first part in a basement off Broadway and now the lead in "Holiday" in stock. She is rising, she is on her way.

*(He hands **ELLEN** reviews.)*

Call publicity, copy these reviews, and send them to our list of producers and casting directors. And write David Merrick, send him this one, and tell him she's right for his new play.

ELLEN. Which one? He's producing six.

GEORGE. The one that's not a British import.

HENRY. *(He opens **GEORGE**'s door.)* Oh, you're back. I am so glad.

GEORGE. *(To **ELLEN**)* Damn, I have so much to tell you.

HENRY. I had to make several important decisions while you were away.

GEORGE. Good. Good.

HENRY. No. They were very bad decisions. And did you read this choice item from Alec Bruin?

(indicates memo he is carrying)

GEORGE. Henry, I just sat down.

HENRY. Well, read it.

(ELLEN's been reading Babcock's reviews, but listening to the boys too. She shows GEORGE the memo. It's from today's batch, and on top.)

ELLEN. There's the Bruin memo, George.

GEORGE. *(to HENRY:)* Oh, he sent you a copy.

HENRY. He sent everyone in America a copy.

GEORGE. My God, he even sent one to Fowler. Why, Henry – this is insulting!

HENRY. Yes. It's also libelous.

GEORGE. *(reading:)* "You boys in the theatre department must learn that our California clients expect the New York ship to be just as ship shape as the Coast ship is." What the hell does that mean?

HENRY. Our ship. It isn't ship shape.

GEORGE. *(turns over memo)* Did I miss something?

HENRY. George, I know it's your first day back, but I...

GEORGE. First day? It's my first minute.

HENRY. Yes, well, Bruin wrote me a memo too, asking me my advice, and we both know that's a trap, so I figured you better answer it and I'll sign my name.

GEORGE. Have you seen my mail?

(holds up a stack of it)

HENRY. I have been through a week of trying to do your work and mine.

GEORGE. Ok. I'll be right in. On Wednesday.

HENRY. George, it's been sitting for days. All right, but make it early Wednesday.

(He exits, back into his office.)

GEORGE. All this mail in a week?

ELLEN. *(still reading reviews)* Life goes on. Hey, Janet's reviews are raves!

GEORGE. I told you! So take a note to the TV department, and tell them I think she's ready for important guest shots. But no series. She wants to live here and take her chances that theatre will keep her busy until feature films open up.

ELLEN. *(writing)* No series.

GEORGE. God, I wish he'd let me hang up her award from last year. "Most Promising Actress."

(He takes the Award from a desk drawer.)

ELLEN. We've been through it. He'll never do that.

GEORGE. It doesn't even clash with the Old English.

(He holds it up next to a print on the wall.)

ELLEN. No one's ever had a plaque on the wall.

GEORGE. This should not be hidden in a drawer.

ELLEN. He wants to see you at eleven o'clock. Today!

GEORGE. OmiGod. You said 'no disasters.'

ELLEN. I thought you needed coffee first.

GEORGE. No, I need blood.

(The phone rings. He talks to it.)

Will you stop that?!

ELLEN. *(into phone:)* Mr. Wilson's office. Yes, he's back.

(hands over phone)

Carl Murray. Will you take it?

GEORGE. Sure. Why not? I have three minutes before my appointment in Samarra.

(into phone:)

Hello, Carl. Oh, you know –

(Hands over phone.)

He knows about Fowler's call.

ELLEN. I didn't tell him.

GEORGE. Right, Carl. I'll call you the minute I come down.

(hangs up)

Isn't it nice to know your every move is up there on the big screen?

ELLEN. Carl *is* head of your department.

GEORGE. *(rummaging through drawers)* Where do I keep my antacid pills?

ELLEN. In your right drawer.

(GEORGE finds them, chews a couple.)

Now don't ask Mr. Fowler about the plaque.

GEORGE. Do you think I'm crazy?

ELLEN. Remember the last time he summoned you?

GEORGE. You know, I don't even remember what he was yelling about. All I remember is he did it in front of three people I'd never met and that later I threw up all over my antique desk.

ELLEN. You know I'm proud of you. But sometimes wouldn't it be wiser to be – accommodating – like everyone else?

GEORGE. Everyone else. Lance is 25 years old, ashamed that he's filthy rich, so he's in deep analysis. Henry brushes his teeth four times a day. We're individuals.

ELLEN. Oh, you're an individual.

GEORGE. What does that mean?

ELLEN. You're a provoker – is that a word? Like that time you came to work wearing a tan suit. That was deliberate.

GEORGE. I didn't know Fearless wanted us to wear black.

ELLEN. Everyone knew. You wore it to provoke him.

GEORGE. And when he caught me in it, and sent me home to change, what did I do?

ELLEN. All right, you changed it. But you came back wearing a flaming red tie.

GEORGE. But he didn't send me home. And that's progress. My victory with the red tie meant a great deal to me. I expect you to understand that, and encourage it.

ELLEN. I do.

GEORGE. How?

ELLEN. Well – your desk, for instance. Didn't I help you move it so it doesn't face the door?

GEORGE. That's no victory!

ELLEN. It's the *only* desk in the agency that doesn't face the door!

GEORGE. Well, that was a step. A tiny step.

ELLEN. Listen to me! Mr. Fowler only comes to New York now and then.

GEORGE. Yeah, well this one of the 'nows.'

ELLEN. But you always manage to provoke him.

GEORGE. Well then you're right, that's what I do. When I went to camp the kids hung me upside down from the rafters. Does that sound like everyone else?

ELLEN. You're making that up. Why?

GEORGE. Because my father wrote me letters in Latin. "Fileus meus; Fatum erit cum tidi." And I understood him.

ELLEN. That wasn't your fault.

GEORGE. I was ten years old in the eighth grade. My best friend, Mervin Marks, threw spitballs at me all through my valedictory speech. Well, I was ten years old, four feet tall, and Latin kept popping out, so why shouldn't they hate me?

ELLEN. You were valedictorian? I wish I'd been there. I would have respected you.

GEORGE. No one respected me. So when they gave me a Phi Beta Kappa key in college I stuck it in a drawer like, you know, I was ashamed. Then one day Fearless sent me home to put on that black suit, and I opened the drawer, and the key popped out, and I thought, "What the hell – it's not a scarlet letter!" So I was a boy genius, and Mervin Marks was a jock, and Charley King could yodel, and Rosalie de Santis always got "A" in deportment. See? We all had *something*. So I picked up the key and decided, "Nuts to that, George. Fight Fearless hard. Every way you can. Every day. And I found me a sassy red tie, and stuck the key through it, and that – that was the start of my fight.

(shows her the key, which he still wears)

See?

(He picks up the framed award, from his desk.)

And this – this could be another step. The first award a client of mine ever gave me. You should have been there the night she won it!

ELLEN. I was. You took me.

GEORGE. Oh. Yes.

ELLEN. In a hired limousine, which you paid for yourself.

GEORGE. Well then you know what it means to me.

ELLEN. It was nice of her to give it to you.

GEORGE. Yeah. But not to stick in a drawer.

ELLEN. Well, don't ask about hanging it today.

GEORGE. I've already asked him once, and he said no.

ELLEN. *(looking at watch)* Not that I'm worried he'll – George, it's eleven o'clock!

GEORGE. What? Oh.

(He opens the tablet box.)

Hey listen, you want an antacid tablet?

(He takes two, and chews.)

ELLEN. No. Well, maybe one.

(She takes one.)

GEORGE. What does Fowler want with me? I was so glad to be back. I have all this mail, and Henry needs me, and I haven't even seen Lance, and I have so many people to call about Babcock, why doesn't he leave me alone!

ELLEN. When you see him, don't talk too much.

GEORGE. What the hell. My suit's the right color. If I'm not back by noon, send Henry up. Tell him not to knock, just come in and separate us.

ELLEN. Now you know what to say when you go in?

GEORGE. I'll say "Oh Fearless Leader, I have come. Do with me what you will."

(The phone rings. **ELLEN** *answers it.)*

ELLEN. Mr. Wilson's office. Martha, he's on his way up now.

(Through the rest of this, **ELLEN** *keeps motioning* **GEORGE** *to get out, but he just smiles back, "No.")*

Well, I know you said eleven o'clock, but it's just two minutes after. George has been out of town covering a client – well, of course he's back. I just told you he's probably in the elevator right now. All right!

(hangs up)

Why did I never learn to say –

(to phone:)

Bitch!

GEORGE. Bitch. That's good. And Felix is a bastard.

ELLEN. Bastard!

GEORGE & ELLEN. *(***GEORGE** *conducts, as an orchestra leader)*
Felix Fowler is a bastard!

(The phone rings.)

The son of a bitch! He heard us!

(He dashes out.)

(BLACKOUT)

Scene 2

(*TIME: Almost an hour later.*)

(*In the dark we hear a phonograph recording of a female vocalist. When the lights come up on George's office,* **HENRY OLDSCHAN** *is listening meditatively, and thumbing through some photographs. Stage right is lit too, and the* **SECRETARIES** *are busy typing, phoning, working. A second or two to establish, then* **LANCE** *emerges from his own office, looks for* **HENRY** *in Henry's office, then immediately enters George's office.*)

LANCE. Henry, what time is it? My watch stopped at eleven.

HENRY. Shhh. An NTA artist.

(*He holds up a headshot.*)

LANCE. She'll have to wait.

(*He turns off the demo.*)

What time is it?

HENRY. It's twelve thirty. Why the panic button?

LANCE. I need twenty dollars by one o'clock.

HENRY. For what?

LANCE. Lunch with Maria Cueva.

HENRY. Oh, no. I don't pay for your love life.

LANCE. This is strictly business. Why do you guys all think of me as a rich young kid with nothing on his mind but women?

HENRY. You figure it out.

LANCE. But I want to make something of my life! Maria Cueva is a well known Mexican actress and she's agreed to audition for NTA. But I've GOT to give her the lunch treatment because I want her to stay in New York and sign with us. Henry, I've never signed anyone!

HENRY. I know. I know. I've wondered about that.

LANCE. Well, it's not easy. I mean if you were an actor, would you want me as your agent?

HENRY. I see your point.

LANCE. Maria doesn't know I'm the bottom of the barrel. All she heard was National Talent Agency, and that she understood. Remember, she speaks very little English.

HENRY. So how does she audition – with gestures?

LANCE. She reads English very well. So I've written her a very simple scene. She'll do it Thursday. But if we don't sign her, she'll go home to Mexico and I'm still the only agent in the world with NO personal clients.

HENRY. Well, why come to me for lunch money? You've got an expense account. Get an advance.

LANCE. I'm allowed three dollars a week! Where could I take her on three dollars?

HENRY. You could go crazy at Chock Full o' Nuts.

LANCE. I told you – in Mexico she's a celebrity.

HENRY. So sell some stocks.

LANCE. My stocks are locked in a vault, and I don't have a key. My father doesn't trust me, and he's right not to. I live on my stinky salary.

HENRY. I've never even been in a bank vault. Could we go over one day and just wander around? I wouldn't touch anything.

LANCE. It'll cost you twenty bucks.

(**HENRY** *hands him the money.*)

HENRY. Ok. You're on. Imagine – me lending you money. You own a townhouse!

LANCE. I own nothing! And even if I did, I can't spend a townhouse. Do you think George would hear her too?

HENRY. Yes, George would hear her. If he still works here on Thursday.

LANCE. Oh boy, it's twelve-thirty, and he's still up with Fowler.

HENRY. Some men have been known to go up and never come down.

LANCE. What does Fowler do? Seal them in the wall?

HENRY. I knew a guy who never came down. I think they shot him out of the building by pneumatic tube.

(**GEORGE** *enters Secretarial area, extreme stage right. As he crosses to his office, he signals* **MILDRED** *and* **ELLEN** *to come with him.*)

LANCE. Don't you think you should go up and see if there's any blood under the door?

HENRY. With Felix, there is never any blood.

(**GEORGE** *and the* **SECRETARIES** *enter his office.*)

GEORGE. Oh good. I want you both too.

LANCE. George, what happened?

GEORGE. It was good. It was very good.

ELLEN. Don't leave anything out. First you opened the door. What office was he in?

GEORGE. He doesn't have an office here. He was using the huge party room. I went in, and he was alone.

HENRY. Sitting on his throne. Was he wearing the crown?

GEORGE. He was behind that enormous desk. There was nothing on it, not even a pencil. At first I couldn't even see him, the light was in my eyes.

MILDRED. He likes that. He likes the light over his head, like a halo.

GEORGE. At first I was nervous. He's never behaved this way with me before.

LANCE. Which way?

GEORGE. Well – he wouldn't take any calls.

ELLEN. No – calls.

GEORGE. Rosalind Russell called. He wouldn't talk to her.

HENRY. No calls! He takes calls in the bathroom!

GEORGE. And I kept thinking, if we're alone, it can't be too bad because if he wants to tear you apart, he always has two or three others standing around to watch.

LANCE. Why does he do that?

GEORGE.	**HENRY.**	**MILDRED.**
Because he's our leader.	Because it's humiliating.	Because he's cru-el.

GEORGE. And sure enough he finally got to the subject: Carol Beaumont.

LANCE. Why would he talk to YOU about HER?

ELLEN. She's coming back to Broadway. It's been in all the papers.

GEORGE. He told me how close he's always been to her.

HENRY. Sure. They picked him to service her on her first picture. He was just like us before that picture.

LANCE. He was like me? Fowler was once – nothing?

HENRY. Lower even than you.

MILDRED. He started in the mailroom.

GEORGE. And how when she won the Oscar, she said right on television that he deserved it as much as she did.

MILDRED. So you strolled down memory lane together. But where was it all leading?

GEORGE. Well – he hadn't decided who should make her deal on the new play.

ELLEN. So?

GEORGE. Who should personally represent her on the east coast.

MILDRED. So?

GEORGE. So. I'm it.

HENRY. You? I mean George, this lady is a very big star.

LANCE. Fearless picked you?

ELLEN. This is the setup for your Vice Presidency.

GEORGE. Well it'll be good for all of us. Cause when it comes off, I'll let him know how helpful you all were.

HENRY. What helpful? My last deal took four weeks to negotiate and the play ran three nights.

GEORGE. That wasn't your fault. You didn't write the play.

HENRY. No, my negotiations were brilliant. THEY should have been reviewed. We'd still be running.

GEORGE. Well, this play will run. She's from Broadway originally you know, this Beaumont. I've seen her onstage and she is magical!

LANCE. And what can I do? I've never made a deal for over $200. I don't know anything about star contracts.

GEORGE. You'll do research. Ellen, get your pad.

(She runs out, gets it from her desk, and immediately returns.)

I've never tackled one as big as this either. Lance, you go up to legal and get me five or six samples of top contracts for Broadway.

*(As **ELLEN** returns, he signals her to note the following.)*

GEORGE. I want language for house seats, transportation out of town, air-conditioned dressing rooms, allowance for personal maid, vacation clauses, the whole works. She's Fowler's personal client, so it'll put us right under his beady little eye.

HENRY. And that's where you want to be?

GEORGE. You're damned right I do. We're the best there is.

LANCE. We really are?

HENRY. What a crummy profession this is!

GEORGE. This is our chance to prove it so don't disappear.

HENRY. Poor Beaumont. The end of a great career.

LANCE. Listen, shouldn't we do something fancy with her billing, like get her a box around her name?

GEORGE. I thought you didn't know anything about big stuff?

LANCE. Oh, I've been around. People tell me I'm apt. I just want you to know I'm avid and zealous too.

MILDRED. Listen avid, zealous and apt – you're already late for lunch.

LANCE. OmiGod. Maria Cueva. If the luncheon goes badly, George – I leave everything to you and Henry.

MILDRED. What about me?

LANCE. *(as he exits:)* You can have my job.

MILDRED. Thanks a bunch.

LANCE. Henry, walk me to the corner. I want to talk about this.

HENRY. *(as he goes:)* I'd better go with him. I don't think he should be out alone.

(He exits too.)

MILDRED. That's just what I need – his job. I already earn twice what he does.

GEORGE. Mildred, you know a lot about contracts, don't you?

MILDRED. Oh, contracts. I've seen a few.

GEORGE. No, really. Star contracts.

MILDRED. *(at the window)* Do you know that skyscraper across the street?

GEORGE. Yeah.

MILDRED. When I first looked out this window, it was a one story kosher delicatessen. That was a lot of contracts ago.

ELLEN. George, you left a lot out. Do you mean you walked in and Mr. Fowler just handed you Carol Beaumont?

GEORGE. No, no – it took him about 40 minutes. I got all the background, and then he sort of slid into his famous "Rise from the ashes" speech, and I didn't know if he meant him, her or me.

MILDRED. He once pulled that speech on Marty Greenhut, who was head of this department. Oh, dear.

ELLEN. Why? What happened to him?

MILDRED. They carted him away. To the Dallas office.

ELLEN. Oh George, he won't send you to Dallas!

MILDRED. No dear, not Dallas. That's full up. Peru maybe.

GEORGE. Now stop that! It's an honor, and I don't want any smart remarks.

MILDRED. Really? What came after the speech?

GEORGE. Nothing. He told me to take over.

MILDRED. As simply as that.

GEORGE. And I told him I was delighted and I was glad I could be of help.

MILDRED. That's what Mr. Greenhut said just before he left for Lima.

GEORGE. Ellen, get me a copy of the play. I want to read it before I meet Beaumont. Oh, and call her producer and set up an appointment for tomorrow. No, let me talk to him – would you get him on the phone?

ELLEN. That's David Merrick, right?

(She dials.)

GEORGE. Right. I sent the boys to get me reference contracts. Mildred, you have any ideas?

MILDRED. Let's see. Lady stars. What's she going to wear in this opus?

GEORGE. I don't know. I came in when you did.

MILDRED. Well, be sure Mr. Merrick pays for her underwear.

GEORGE. Her what?

MILDRED. I remember one star who said she could only play her part in silk panties – she simply could not create her character without them – and she didn't personally wear silk panties – so it was the producer's responsibility to supply them. He didn't agree. Carl Murray was her agent. He won that battle, but it wasn't pretty.

GEORGE. Her panties are part of my job?

MILDRED. Just call them 'undergarments.' That'll cover everything.

ELLEN. *(on the phone, a little grand:)* Mr. Merrick, please. George Wilson calling from NTA about Carol Beaumont's contract.

GEORGE. That sounds good.

*(to **MILDRED**:)*

Anything else?

MILDRED. What's her billing?

GEORGE. Sole star above the title.

MILDRED. One hundred percent size type?

GEORGE. Of course. She's Carol Beaumont.

(He takes out the antacid pill bottle from his desk.)

MILDRED. Make sure it's 100% the size of the largest letter of the title. Especially with Merrick. He had a show once where he made the first letter of the title enormous, and everything that followed teeny tiny, and he billed the star 100% the size of the tiny part. There was a chaserai about that, I can tell you.

GEORGE. *(taking notes)* Mildred, you are a genius.

(pops a pill in his mouth)

ELLEN. *(into phone:)* I'll hold, thank you.

GEORGE. You should be the agent.

MILDRED. *(picks up pill bottle, looks at it)* What's the matter, don't you like me? Now let's see, what else can we stick him with?

ELLEN. *(into phone:)* Mr. Merrick?! Just a moment, sir.

*(She hands **GEORGE** the phone.)*

GEORGE. Hello, Mr. Merrick. I'm George Wilson. – No, we haven't met, but I'm going to be making Carol Beaumont's deal with you –

(He laughs.)

That's very funny.

MILDRED. I'll bet.

GEORGE. *(laughs again)* I never knew you were a humorist.

MILDRED. What humorist? He hasn't smiled since his mother died.

ELLEN. Shhh! That's David Merrick!

MILDRED. Honey, I've known him since he was David Margulies. Silence from me he doesn't get.

ELLEN. Mildred, please. George is very nervous.

(GEORGE, listening, laughs again.)

MILDRED. No, he's not. He should be. But he's not.

GEORGE. Well, we'll talk it all out tomorrow. I'll be over around three o'clock. Nice talking to you. Goodbye.

(hangs up)

Well, this is going to be fun. Imagine, I call David Merrick, he talks to me.

ELLEN. What was so funny?

GEORGE. He was charming. He told me he didn't want Beaumont in his play. He was just accommodating the director, who does want her. He told me not to come over if she wanted more than $400 a week.

MILDRED. He must want her. That's a lot from him for openers.

GEORGE. He called her a broken down has been who can't get arrested in Hollywood.

MILDRED. Yes, that's David. So respectful.

GEORGE. So he's a diamond in the rough. I can handle that.

MILDRED. No. More like a toadstool in the rough.

GEORGE. Mildred, have faith. It's the beginning of a new era.

(CARL MURRAY opens the door, and enters.)

CARL. Ah, George – you are back.

MILDRED. Well, good luck with your new era. Just light some candles, pray a lot and get everything in writing.

(as she exits)

Hello, Mr. Murray.

CARL. Mildred. George, I need some time.

ELLEN. You don't need me?

(GEORGE nods 'no.' ELLEN exits.)

CARL. Didn't you promise to call me after your meeting upstairs?

GEORGE. I'm sorry. But talk about crazy Mondays.

CARL. Thanks a lot. What did he say?

GEORGE. He gave me the Beaumont contract.

CARL. I know that. Did he mention me?

GEORGE. You know? How do you know?

CARL. He called me right after you left him. Did my name come up at all?

GEORGE. No. No, it didn't.

CARL. You didn't listen to me. Can't I make you understand this is "selection time." And we must be very careful.

GEORGE. Do you think you have a chance?

CARL. Does it seem so strange to you?

GEORGE. No. Not that you should be picked. Only that you should talk to me about it.

CARL. I think you should know I once talked to Felix about it.

GEORGE. You did?

CARL. He told me that Vice Presidents were picked by the Board of Directors, and that the titles were bestowed as a privilege. He didn't like my asking.

GEORGE. Felix Fowler the First.

CARL. He was right. He told me to be patient.

GEORGE. When was that?

CARL. Last year. Well, I've been patient, but it's time again. And now he gives Beaumont to you. I should be angry, George – I FOUND Beaumont, I saw her in a school play, twenty years ago, and I signed her to NTA. Until she went into films, I did all her contracts in the theatre. But I'm not angry.

GEORGE. Jesus Carl, if I'd known she was your client, I'd never have let him put me on this.

CARL. She is not my client, and don't ever say that again! Felix asked for you because he obviously feels you're the one to do it best.

GEORGE. Don't you ever stop defending him? Even when he hurts you?

CARL. He needs no defense from me. Without him there'd be no Carol Beaumont for you to cut your teeth on, no NTA initials after your name, which believe me open more doors for you than you know.

GEORGE. But he passed over you. He gave her to me!

CARL. Yes. And why do you suppose he did that?

GEORGE. Have I got something to do with that too?

CARL. You've been away a week. Where?

GEORGE. You know where. In Columbus with Janet Babcock. I told you I was going.

CARL. You said Columbus. I thought you'd be back overnight.

GEORGE. I was in Ohio, it made sense to scout other stock companies. I must have seen six plays.

CARL. And there was no one worth signing.

GEORGE. No. But there might have been.

CARL. Might have beens don't interest me. All Felix knows is you spent two hundred dollars to service one client who earns us ten cents.

GEORGE. Did he complain to you about that?

CARL. All I said was he knows you went.

GEORGE. But she's developing, Carl. She's playing star parts. I can't advise her on what's next if I don't see her work.

CARL. Felix wants us to sign, service and sell. You signed Babcock last March.

GEORGE. And a dozen before her. All of whom are doing just fine.

CARL. But no one since last March.

GEORGE. She's good. The good ones are hard to find. If you want to be there when the break comes, when they become interesting to those charmers on the west coast, you have to support them while they're struggling.

CARL. You spend too much time on them; you only spoil them.

GEORGE. What should I do? Sign them by the pound?

CARL. You should have signed someone.

GEORGE. I've looked in every cellar and school that ever did a play. You used to come with me. You said we were the Tiffany of the business. Why do we need a long list of deadheads? For Christ's sake, you taught me that!

CARL. Felix doesn't come East often, and when he does, he doesn't want philosophy, he wants results, he asks questions.

GEORGE. So? I have answers.

CARL. He doesn't ask you. He asks me.

GEORGE. I'm not hiding behind you.

CARL. I'm still responsible for you. He's left me that. I'm still responsible.

GEORGE. So it's Felix again, huh? You've got it figured out that because I went to Ohio for a week, foolishly in your eyes, he passed you up to punish you, and gave Beaumont to me. Well, that's far too complicated for me. I'm just a little boy from Bayonne and that's much too Madison Avenue big city fancy talk to me. So I think I got Beaumont because Felix wanted me to have her. No tricks. No strings. I'm right for her, she's right for me. Now what do you think about that?

CARL. You are dumber than hell.

GEORGE. That's your answer?

CARL. Yes. Because you're not handling Carol Beaumont alone.

GEORGE. What?!

CARL. Alec Bruin's in on it too. He's come east. He's here, to help you.

GEORGE. Help me what?

CARL. Bruin has serviced Carol Beaumont on her last three pictures. He knows her, she likes him. You don't like him. But she does.

GEORGE. Fearless makes her deals himself. Himself! She's his personal client. What does Bruin do? Have her photos developed? See that she has milk in her coffee?

CARL. He handled all the details, worked out the refinements on her movie deals. He's very close to her, and now he's going to share your office, and help you with this play.

GEORGE. Fearless didn't tell me that.

CARL. Well he told me. I am the head of this department, George. He called me himself and he told me.

GEORGE. When does the fun begin?

CARL. Today.

GEORGE. Dammit, I would have said no. You want me in the spotlight? OK. But don't stick Bruin in there with me. Not Bruin!

CARL. George, it's your deal. Felix said so.

GEORGE. Sure it's my deal.

CARL. I tell you it is. You'll do the booking report, you'll get the credit. What the hell does Alec know about the theatre?

GEORGE. He knows a lot. He *told* me not to sign Barbra Streisand.

CARL. He's just going to hold Carol's hand. You know, advise on the little things.

GEORGE. Advise, hell. He's going to sit on this side of my desk and drive me out of my mind.

CARL. He'll help you. You're not used to movie stars. Beaumont's tough. Alec will help you.

GEORGE. Fowler couldn't even tell me to my face. Don't you see what he's doing? It's like Isabella sends Columbus to prove the earth is round. But she sticks a rowboat in front of the Santa Maria to warn him just in case it's not. And Bruin's in the rowboat. Well, damn it, I don't want any rowboats. If anyone's going to fall off, it's going to be me!

CARL. God damn it, you're babbling! Bruin knows this woman and you don't. You sound like a petulant child, stamping his foot. He can help you! What's the big deal?

GEORGE. I'm sorry my well known quiet charm isn't cutting it with you. You and our leader feel I'll be more effective with a nursemaid. And what happens when I get out of town with 'my client' and she asks me what I thought of the first act re-writes, and whether her dress is the right color, is her leadintg man too young for her and what should be done about the second act curtain, which isn't a curtain at all? What do I do, wire Bruin to find out what I think? How do I get her to listen to me if Bruin and I go waltzing hand in hand through the preliminaries? Come on, Carl, I'm listening.

CARL. Will you relax? Roll with the punches a little. Someone's going to be appointed and Jesus wouldn't it be nice if it were me? We did spend three years together, Felix knows I trained you. So do this right, huh?

GEORGE. I don't know what to do.

CARL. Use Alec. Please, George – do it Felix's way just one time. I don't want to be passed over again.

GEORGE. I don't know.

CARL. Come on – smile a little. It's a break for you. I should congratulate you. We should have a drink on it.

GEORGE. Carl, leave me alone, huh?

CARL. Well, you take one. It'll do you good.

GEORGE. I don't want to drink. I want to think.

CARL. Sure. Call me, George. I want to know each step as it happens. I'm still the boss, right? Call me, George.

(He exits.)

(**GEORGE** *rings his desk buzzer twice. He takes scotch bottle out of desk drawer, pours, takes a sip, makes a face. He hates the taste.* **ELLEN** *enters.*)

ELLEN. Oh, boy.

GEORGE. *(indicating scotch)* What, this? You're going to see a lot more of this.

ELLEN. Do you still have the Beaumont deal?

GEORGE. Boy, did I have me fooled!

ELLEN. You lost it.

GEORGE. No, we're playing halfies. Alec Bruin has the other half.

ELLEN. He's coming here?

GEORGE. He *is* here. Well, so what? I can handle him!

(pours another drink)

Don't you see? Wearing a red tie and moving my desk – I could hide behind those the rest of my life here and convince myself I wasn't being cloned. That's all just the banks of the river. I have to get in the middle, over my head, and swim.

ELLEN. I have no idea what you're talking about, but I have three words for you. Don't do it.

GEORGE. Don't say 'don't' to me.

ELLEN. They're not going to send you to Dallas or Peru. They're going to fire you.

GEORGE. So what? I can always get a job. I was the best damned dish washer NYU ever had.

ELLEN. And I sold cookies for the Girl Scouts. But that is not a life's work!

GEORGE. You know, it's funny, but I'm beginning to feel up again!

ELLEN. Well, I don't like it. You're getting that "I am different" look. You're getting that kind of crazy "I am me" star in your eye.

GEORGE. Don't throw cold water. Don't ask questions. Just come along with me.

ELLEN. I don't know where you're going!

GEORGE. Neither do I!

ELLEN. So that's how I am – I have to ask!

GEORGE. I'm suddenly very hungry. That's a good sign. Come on kid, I'll buy you a hamburger.

ELLEN. Ok. I'll just get my purse.

(She reacts to the pointedness of Gloria's earlier remark.

She looks longingly after **GEORGE** *as he disappears into his washroom off left, only partially closing the door. She moves into the Secretarial Area, closing George's door behind her. Lights up on Secretarial Area, and remain on in George's office.)*

(**ELLEN** *goes to closet, gets her purse.*)

ELLEN. *(continued)* Gloria, can we bring you something?

GLORIA. No thanks, I'm still on the baby food.

ELLEN. We're just going to grab a hamburger.

GLORIA. Ellen, did I waste my breath?

ELLEN. What can I do?

(She waves, and runs smack into the arms of **ALEC BRUIN**, *as he enters, stage right.)*

Oh! Excuse me.

(She exits. **ALEC** *moves in, carrying a small suitcase.)*

ALEC. *(to the departing* **ELLEN**:*)* That's all right, my fault really.

GLORIA. Can I help you?

ALEC. If you're Ellen Wolsky, I'm your new better half.

GLORIA. I'm Gloria West. Ellen was the one who just left. And you are?

ALEC. Brother Bruin. In the flesh.

GLORIA. Ooooh. I've talked to you so many times, on the tie line. But I never pictured Alec Bruin like you – I mean you SOUND so much older.

ALEC. I know. Everyone says that. Actually, I'm only 57.

GLORIA. Oooh. A funny one.

ALEC. I'm sharing George Wilson's office for a while. Is he in?

GLORIA. I haven't seen him. Should I check?

ALEC. No need.

GLORIA. Well, his door's closed, so if he's in, I'm supposed to check.

ALEC. I'm Brother Bruin – we're family.

*(at **GEORGE**'s door)*

Oh, would you get me David Merrick on the phone?

GLORIA. All right.

*(**GLORIA** looks annoyed, but shakes it off, and sits down to dial. **ALEC** moves into **GEORGE**'s office, and starts to unpack his bag. The first things out are golf shoes. He notices the scotch on the desk, and begins rummaging through George's drawers. **GLORIA** enters suddenly.)*

Mr. Bruin. Your phone call's ready.

ALEC. Don't you girls knock before entering a room?

GLORIA. I didn't think you'd like it. You know, me being family.

ALEC. Which line is Mr. Merrick on?

GLORIA. 52.

ALEC. Thank you, Gloria. Ciao.

(She leaves, goes back to her desk. He picks up the phone.)

Mr. Merrick! Hello there, this is Alec Bruin at NTA. I'm Carol Beaumont's agent and I'd like so very much to come see you tomorrow about her deal for your beautiful play. — Oh, Mr. Wilson did? Well, that's fine. Three o'clock. Good – Oh no, of course he was authorized to make the appointment. I'm just a California boy when it comes to the theatre. I'll make the deal with you, and George will handle the details and work out the refinements. He's going to assist me; he's my assistant. – Well, thank you sir, we'll see you tomorrow.

*(He hangs up. **GLORIA** knocks on the door.)*

Come!

GLORIA. Are you sure I can't be of any help?

ALEC. No. What time is it?

GLORIA. One o'clock.

ALEC. Oh boy, I'm late. Tell you what, call Mr. Fowler.

(He starts to exit.)

GLORIA. Me? Call Mr Fowler!

ALEC. Tell Martha I'm on my way up for lunch.

GLORIA. You're having lunch with him?

ALEC. That's right.

GLORIA. Ooooh. What in the world do you talk about?

ALEC. Well, I've only been here five minutes. But don't you worry. I'll think of something.

*(**GLORIA** sits at her desk, and dials, giving her message quietly. Suddenly, on stage left, the washroom door opens and **GEORGE** comes out, slightly dazed. He's heard everything. He calmly moves to his desk, takes out the antacid pills. He takes one, chews it, and pours more to take with him. He walks quietly out of his office, and into the Secretarial Area. **GLORIA** looks up, surprised.)*

GLORIA. George! I thought you were out to lunch.

GEORGE. No. I was burping in the bathroom.

GLORIA. I haven't even seen you to say 'hello.' Did you have a good trip? Did you have a pleasant Monday morning? I'll bet you're glad to be back!

*(**GEORGE** stops, turns, gives her a murderous look. He stares for a moment, then bursts into tears, and exits.)*

(CURTAIN)

ACT II

*(**SETTING**: The same.)*

*(**TIME**: Thursday morning.)*

*(**AT RISE**: **GEORGE** is seated behind his desk, almost buried under a pile of contracts, reference books, etc. **ELLEN** is seated between George's chair and a third chair, a new one opposite **GEORGE**. **ALEC BRUIN** is Upstage Center, standing on his head, with his feet propped against the wall for support.)*

ALEC. Forty six – forty seven – forty eight – forty nine – fifty.

(He upends himself, brushes himself off.)

Nothing like it. Brother Wilson, New York is no place for a man who likes exercise.

GEORGE. You could try walking.

ALEC. A Californian walk? I don't think so.

GEORGE. I walk all the time – after work.

ALEC. Don't let Felix hear you say "after work."

ELLEN. Would you like to finish this letter, Mr. Bruin? You had started a letter before you were suddenly upside down.

ALEC. Oh, yes. Where was I?

ELLEN. It's to Mrs. Fowler, and you were telling her all about New York.

ALEC. Right. "So I hope Felix sends me home soon. Meanwhile, don't forget to water that orange tree I gave you." Ok, Ellen, that's it.

ELLEN. Any copies, Mr. Bruin?

ALEC. Mr. Bruin's my father. No – no copies. Oh, and don't put your initials at the bottom. It's a personal note.

ELLEN. Do you want to sign it – "sincerely"?

ALEC. Uh, no. "Fondly":

ELLEN. "Fondly." Fine.

(She prepares to leave.)

GEORGE. Ellen, I expect Maria Cueva at eleven to audition. Put her in Lance's office, and tell Mildred and Carl I'd like them to hear her too.

ELLEN. All right.

(She exits.)

ALEC. How's the contract coming?

GEORGE. We have a draft.

ALEC. We made a good deal, didn't we?

GEORGE. *(The phone rings on his desk.)* Hello. Oh, just a minute.

*(It's **ELLEN** on the intercom. He hands the phone to **ALEC**).*

It's for you.

ALEC. Who is it?

GEORGE. *(into phone:)* Who is it, Ellen?

*(Then, to **ALEC:**)*

Wow! It's Warren Beatty.

ALEC. Is he in New York?

GEORGE. *(into phone:)* Where's he calling from?

*(To **ALEC:**)*

Uh, huh.

ALEC. Tell her to keep him busy for a minute.

*(**ALEC** grabs the phone on his side of the desk, and dials.)*

GEORGE. Yes, sir!

(into phone:)

Ellen, could you hold him on? Don't be nervous. Tell him how much you liked "Splendor In The Grass." – Now calm down – it's good practice. Some day, who knows, a movie star may call us!

(He pushes the 'hold' button. Then, to **ALEC:**)

And what are you doing?

ALEC. *(into the second phone)* Harvey, Alec Bruin. When did Warren Beatty get to town? What hotel? Did you get him tickets for any shows? Is he alone, or with Julie? How long's he due to stay? – Right.

(He hangs up, and pushes the other button, the one Beatty is waiting on.)

Warren Beatty, you old son of a gun. This is Brother Bruin. – So you sneaked in "Mame" without me – Well, I'll admit Julie's prettier than I am, but you might have let me know you were in town. – I sat home alone, watching the Late Show when we could have been out doubling – Now let's see, you're leaving town tonight so there's no get-together, right? – Well sure, Warren, of course we'll do it. No trouble at all – Love to Julie. See you on the Coast.

(He hangs up.)

GEORGE. Do you do that all the time? Or was that just for me?

ALEC. *(pays no attention; he's already dialed another extension on the phone)* Harvey, Bruin again. Now look man, the next time a star gets to town you let me know *before* he calls or I'll have your ass in a sling. – Never mind Henry Oldschan knew, I didn't know. I am the motion picture department and it's your simple job to see that I do know. – Now get a boy over to the Drake Hotel, pick up Mr. Beatty's film, have it developed, and ship it to him in Beverly Hills. And hop to it.

(He hangs up.)

GEORGE. Again, wow!

ALEC. What wow? Is developing film any more demeaning than fighting over silk panties?

GEORGE. I don't mean the film. I mean the other part about your sitting home alone. Would it have been so awful to say "Hello, Warren baby – I didn't know you were in town."

ALEC. Oh, that. No, that wouldn't have been good. They like to think you care.

GEORGE. You do realize you just made four statements in which every word was a lie?

ALEC. What lie? He did all those things.

GEORGE. But you made it sound like you'd arranged it all.

ALEC. So now he feels loved and wanted. Is that bad?

GEORGE. But you went to the theatre last night. Suppose he'd seen you when you were supposed to be home with Johnny Carson.

ALEC. He rented a limousine, I took a taxi, we were at different shows. How could he see me?

GEORGE. You're *funnier* than Johnny Carson!

ALEC. Don't make jokes. I was a good agent.

GEORGE. Yeah? Who says?

ALEC. As a matter of fact, Felix says. It's in his book.

GEORGE. Felix wrote a book?!

ALEC. I'm surprised you've never read it. What I just did? It's all there – in Chapter Three. "What Star Clients Will Expect."

GEORGE. Well, I hope Carol Beaumont doesn't expect me to play Chapter Three all through the run.

ALEC. A friendly tip. Read the book.

GEORGE. Because I'm not good at games, even when I like them. And I don't like the one you just played.

ALEC. Then learn to like it. If you want to breathe that finer air up top, you're going to have to learn that these good folks who pay us ten percent of a fortune like to be spoiled just a wee bit. And you don't make the rules Brother Wilson, they do.

GEORGE. Different folks, different strokes.

ALEC. I've heard you were peculiar.

GEORGE. Right! Like I like a direct answer once in a while. And while we're on that subject, why the hell don't you ever answer my memos? Or my phone calls?

ALEC. I do. Eventually. But the clients come first.

GEORGE. Like having their film developed?

ALEC. A poor choice, but even that is more important that answering your memos about Janet Babcock, who earns this company about forty dollars a year.

GEORGE. Well, I'll be Goddamned! She's a client! Just like Mr. Beatty. And by the way, he once earned us $40 a year too. Carl Murray handled him right up to when your precious Coast started paying attention to him. And my memos are not concerned with printing her snapshots. If you read them once in a while, you'd learn that.

ALEC. When Janet Babcock earns three hundred thousand a flick, I'll answer over night. In the meantime, give me a draft of the contract. Felix expects me up with it.

GEORGE. *(hands it to him, keeps one copy for himself)* Don't let me keep you.

ALEC. OK, I'm off to see the wizard. Brother Wilson, I'll be sure to give him your regards. Ciao.

*(**ALEC** exits. **GEORGE**, angry, buzzes for **ELLEN**. When she doesn't appear at once...)*

GEORGE. Wolsky!

(She appears.)

ELLEN. You're angry. What happened?

GEORGE. If he calls me "Brother" one more time I'm going to deck him.

ELLEN. That's just a quirk of his.

GEORGE. Is that what it is?

ELLEN. Show some self control.

GEORGE. Why should I?

ELLEN. Come on George, you know you think of him as the enemy.

GEORGE. Do you think I met him the day we shook hands? You can tell something about a man from his memos and I've had five long years of those.

ELLEN. That's business, George. He may be charming outside the office.

GEORGE. Leopards don't change spots, I'm told.

ELLEN. I think he might.

GEORGE. What?!

ELLEN. I think it would be nice to have a date with an attractive guy to find out what he's like.

GEORGE. As opposed to what you and I go out on?

ELLEN. You and I? I don't mean dinner at Nedick's and then Ionesco on Bleeker Street followed by coffee with four scratchy actors. I don't mean lunch on the way to a 1:30 audition. I mean Jones Beach or Lincoln Center with reserved seats, and if I'm lucky, the odd Monday night at Bloomingdale's.

GEORGE. A department store on a date?

ELLEN. Don't pretend you've forgotten. I got you there once.

GEORGE. I'm not pretending.

ELLEN. Eighteen rooms they put together so young people could see how to furnish with imagination and taste. You took one look and fled to the Men's Room. I had to send someone in to get you.

GEORGE. I was sick!

ELLEN. The exhibit ran six weeks, George. Did you once suggest we go back?

GEORGE. I don't like to look at furniture. Really, I got sick.

ELLEN. Do you think I like sitting through movies I've seen before?

GEORGE. What movies?

ELLEN. Well – "The Bible."

GEORGE. We had two clients in that. You'd seen that before?

ELLEN. All four hours of it.

GEORGE. Why didn't you tell me? It cost seven bucks!

ELLEN. You don't know what I'm talking about, do you?

GEORGE. I'm not a mindreader. How am I supposed to know what you want to do if you don't tell me?

ELLEN. You're supposed to know. When you care about someone, you're supposed to know. Like Alec. Did you know he's an excellent fisherman?

GEORGE. No!

ELLEN. Did you know that bergalls and cunners are a pain in the neck if you're looking for blackfish? And "hackleheads." What about them?

GEORGE. I have no idea. What's a hacklehead?

ELLEN. A scavenger, a parasite, and a sneak.

GEORGE. You mean Alec?

ELLEN. George!

GEORGE. How do you know he's caught cunnals and bergers?

ELLEN. Cunners and bergalls. He told me – at lunch.

GEORGE. You had lunch with that – that hacklehead?

ELLEN. Yes. Well, not exactly. I was sitting in the drug store, there were no other tables, and he asked if he could join me. And before I'd finished my cottage cheese, we were discussing deep sea fishing in the Pacific.

GEORGE. Alfred Hitchcock probably fishes. That's why he knows.

ELLEN. That's not true. He was interested in me.

GEORGE. I'll bet he was.

ELLEN. And it felt just fine. I've known you for three years, and have we ever discussed fishing once? Or Queen Anne, or Mayor Wagner or closet space or Spencer Tracy, to name just a few subjects in which I'm interested? No. We've discussed your critics' prize plaque, and the Dow Jones averages, and your chronic athlete's foot.

GEORGE. I never knew you wanted to talk about fish. Only once you asked me to go fishing.

ELLEN. Right, and I remember your answer.

GEORGE. So do I. It was the truth. I'm not fond of worms.

ELLEN. That shouldn't matter. You have to try. You know what's lacking with us, George? There's this terrible lack of urgency, that's what's lacking. If I weren't here, you'd miss the secretary, but you'd never miss the woman. You actually take me places and forget I was there!

GEORGE. Come on, when did I ever do that?

ELLEN. You're always recommending movies to me, that we've seen together!

GEORGE. Well, when we go out on business, I guess I concentrate on the show.

ELLEN. When we go out on business? There are 52 Saturday nights a year George. Have we ever spent ONE together?

GEORGE. Wasn't the Babcock Award dinner on a Saturday night?

ELLEN. I mean you and me, without even one rotten client. It's like a terrible feeling of being alone. And when you're with someone all the time and you're still alone – oh, George – that's the worst.

GEORGE. So what am I supposed to do?

ELLEN. Nothing. There are no 'supposed to's' here. But I'm going out with Alec Bruin tonight to find out what I've been missing.

GEORGE. Tonight? You asked him out tonight?

ELLEN. He asked me! What do you think I've been talking about?

GEORGE. I thought you meant some day. If he asked you, like next year.

ELLEN. Well he asked me. For tonight.

GEORGE. Oh. Well, if you like that – sort of man – I guess that's all right.

ELLEN. What sort of man?

GEORGE. Well, you know – like you said – a hacklehead.

ELLEN. You are a loner. You do not exactly give away very much of George Wilson. You lend little pieces by the afternoon or evening, but we could see each other all day and seven nights a week and I would get to share nothing with you but your time. I know Alec three days and at least he was interested enough in something outside of himself to find out that I fish and to sneak the subject into our conversation.

GEORGE. I can see that. At sneaking I think he'd be first rate.

ELLEN. Ohh!

GEORGE. He probably knows our Fearless Leader likes you, and he was just buttering you up.

ELLEN. Well, that does it. It that's what you think of me, then it's a good thing we finally had this all out right here and now!

(She moves toward the door.)

GEORGE. It's not what I think of you. It's what I think of him. Ellen!

(But she has gone out the door, and back to the Pool. Lights out on George's office, lights up on stage right area. **MILDRED** *is at her desk very busy poring over papers.* **GLORIA** *is not onstage.)*

ELLEN. My God, Mildred, the time I've wasted! And I behaved like a shrew with him.

MILDRED. You? A shrew?

ELLEN. I know you're supposed to get these things off your chest – it's healthy and all that. But then why do I have – oh, such indigestion?

MILDRED. It's all too much. Lance has been coaching Miss Cueva three times a day and he's getting absolutely nowhere. Stanislavsky he will never be.

ELLEN. Poor Lance, but it's not my problem.

MILDRED. No, it's mine! "Mildred," he says, "go through my address book and put it in alphabetical order. Eighty-five girls in eleven countries, and he sits inside reading Spanish newspapers.

ELLEN. Maybe I went too far with George. Just because he was so angry that I'm going out with Alec. I mean I walked out as though I didn't care.

MILDRED. Didn't care. You waxed his desk with lemon oil this morning.

ELLEN. And I think I pulled the rug right out from under him.

MILDRED. It'll shake him up. He might be shocked enough to propose.

ELLEN. What if he did?

MILDRED. Honey, you've seen the Purex Specials for women on the small screen? After thirty, we are in trouble. I mean I've been in trouble for years and I didn't need Purex to tell me. But you're not over the hill yet kid, and it's time you got yourself a real boyfriend.

ELLEN. Well, this boyfriend is not interested. Just think about him for a minute. He has an apartment with a friendly maid who cleans twice a week. They only communicate by phone so it's a beautiful relationship and it gets stronger every year.

MILDRED. A man and his maid is not the same as a man and his wife. A man with a maid is better off than a man with a wife, but they are not the same.

ELLEN. And when she isn't there to cook for him, he's in there himself whipping up brochettes and ragouts and soufflés.

MILDRED. The little bastard cooks too??

ELLEN. In teflon pans. Which I'd never heard of. Pans – where the food never sticks.

MILDRED. He knows about teflon??

ELLEN. He knows!

MILDRED. Isn't marriage supposed to consummate love? To hell with Purex, I read *that* in McCalls!

ELLEN. You know how he skis in the winter? Well, Vermont is very far away, very cold, and full of rum toddies and girls in well filled stretch pants.

MILDRED. That's not love, kitten. That's old friend s-e-x.

ELLEN. I'll tell him.

MILDRED. I still say get a proposal. You can smooth out the rough edges some other time.

ELLEN. It's more than rough edges. It's a whole basic flaw in him. He's afraid of intimacy.

MILDRED. Now you sound like you once read a book.

ELLEN. That's why books are written. We can learn from them.

MILDRED. Theory, maybe. Not practice. How do I know? I have an enormous library. And a single bed.

ELLEN. Mildred, you're not discussing this.

MILDRED. Do you know what it's taken me a lot of years to learn? If you see a guy you like, don't try to re-arrange him. Not until you've been married two or three weeks.

ELLEN. That's your advice?

MILDRED. Someone should profit from my mistakes. Why not you?

ELLEN. Because everyone has to make her own.

MILDRED. Now you sound like your mother.

ELLEN. I know. She sends me articles.

MILDRED. On what?

ELLEN. *(picks up some from her desk)* "How To Have Children," "How NOT to Have Children." Anything that expresses her point of view.

MILDRED. I thought my mother was a problem because she snores.

ELLEN. I think I yelled at George because of the one that said,

(She reads:)

"Early in the relationship, make him notice you." Well, he noticed me, all right. And I was better off before.

(She puts the article back on her desk.)

MILDRED. But he's jealous. That's good.

ELLEN. He's also furious. And I'm supposed to be riddled with guilt. Well, I am.

MILDRED. Of course you are.

ELLEN. From now on, you want a date? Ask me a whole day in advance. What am I – the booby prize? I have a damned good figure, and I can balance my own checkbook, which is more than he can do.

MILDRED. If you'll stop with the lecture, I was only pointing out that I hear the first animal noises from the little darling. Now if that doesn't please you, then by all means go out with Alec the Rat.

ELLEN. Don't call him that!

MILDRED. I don't like him, or trust him. If you do, and it works out, I'll come to the wedding. I'll wear black, but I'll come. Now leave me alone – I'm busy rewriting the phone book.

ELLEN. I'm going to wash my face.

*(**GLORIA** enters, with coffee.)*

GLORIA. Hi, girls. Coffee time.

MILDRED. *(to* **ELLEN:***)* Good idea. And take a tranquilizer.

ELLEN. I may take two.

(She exits.)

GLORIA. *(indicating* **LANCE***'s office)* How's he holding up?

(The buzzer rings on **MILDRED***'s desk.)*

MILDRED. Yes, Lance. – No, the accent's on the second syllable. "Hablamos la lingua." Quite all right. De nada.

(Hangs up.)

That's how he's holding up.

(Now **MARIA CUEVA** *enters. She is young, volatile, attractive. She speaks some English, but don't count on it.)*

MARIA. Good morning, ladies. I am here. I am Maria Cueva.

MILDRED. Oh, yes, Ms. Cueva. Buenas dias. You're to wait in Mr. Packard's office.

MARIA. I am very nervous. My English no es muy bueno. Ah! – No is very good.

MILDRED. What scene are you doing? Something from "Man of La Mancha"?

MARIA. Oh, no! Mr. Packard wrote it for me special. So I could show off all my – how you say it?

MILDRED. Well, I don't know dear. Just what did you want to show?

MARIA. He says I should show my whole – range.

MILDRED. Oh – your range. I see.

MARIA. Mr. Packard said only five minutes. He will read with me. Cinco minutos. It is very difficult to show very much in cinco minutos.

MILDRED. That depends on how large your range is. Shall we go in?

*(**MARIA** and **MILDRED** go into Lance's office. **CARL MURRAY** enters.)*

CARL. Hello, Gloria. Is George in?

GLORIA. I don't know, Mr. Murray.

CARL. Don't bother to check. I'll just pop in.

*(He goes to **GEORGE**'s door, knocks.)*

GEORGE. *(from his darkened office)* Come on in.

*(**CARL** moves into George's office. Lights up on it, and down on Secretarial Pool. **GEORGE** is at his desk, back to audience, staring out the window.)*

CARL. George. George, it's me – Carl.

GEORGE. *(doesn't turn around)* Hello Carl.

CARL. Are you all right?

GEORGE. No. But nobody cares.

CARL. I do. What's the matter?

GEORGE. *(Turns around to face him. **GEORGE** has the scotch bottle in his hand, and a glass.)* I'm a loner, Carl. Do you know what that is? That's a bad thing to be.

CARL. It that scotch?!

GEORGE. It's not lemonade.

CARL. What are you celebrating?

GEORGE. The end of George as we all knew and loved him. Carl, teach me how to drink.

CARL. What?!

GEORGE. You're so good at it. I'm 31. I should be able to drink more than Ovaltine.

CARL. Well, George – I don't know.

GEORGE. No, I mean you're really good. Three martini lunches; if I had three martinis I'd fall down.

CARL. I admit I always thought you were a little stuffy about me, because after all, George, this is a tough business and a drink now and then just puts a little steam in the old caboose.

GEORGE. That's it Carl, you got it! My caboose is fresh out of steam, so let's have a lesson in "How To."

(He pours a drink for **CARL**, *and another for himself. He hands one to* **CARL.***)*

Now. Really. What have I been doing wrong?

CARL. I think your attitude's wrong. If you're going to fight it, it's just going to reject you.

GEORGE. No, I have rejection already. I'm your friend, little scotch.

(He sips.)

CARL. *(swallowing half of his)* There, that's better. How did that feel?

GEORGE. Well, now that we're friends, I still think anything including witch hazel *tastes* better. But it does travel well. Let's try it again.

(He sips again. **CARL** *finishes his and pours himself another.)*

CARL. Don't gulp it like it's something you want to get behind you. Easy does it.

GEORGE. It's no good. I'm fading.

CARL. Nonsense.

GEORGE. And I'm leaking, too. See? I'm leaking scotch on my copy of Carol Beaumont's contract.

CARL. She has scales and spits fire, you know.

GEORGE. So? Everyone around here does that.

CARL. What are you talking about?

GEORGE. Oh, come on. Suddenly to Ellen I'm a loner? Bruin's not here three days. He's out smooching with my girl because he knows Fowler's fond of her.

CARL. What are you afraid of? That he'll hurt her?

GEORGE. Exactly. Yes.

CARL. Since when do you concern yourself with other people's getting hurt?

GEORGE. What does that mean?

CARL. Three days I've waited for you to tell me how the Beaumont contract is progressing. Or did you forget I came to visit you Monday morning?

GEORGE. You know I would have called if I'd had a problem. But – I didn't.

CARL. I would have liked the call anyway.

GEORGE. I've had Brother Bruin's advice and counsel.

CARL. Was he helpful?

GEORGE. Oh, very. He joined me at David Merrick's office Tuesday, and told us he'd seen a play the night before that put him to sleep. "Oh," said Mr. Merrick, "which one?" So Brother Bruin said "I can't even remember the title, but it's that piece of drivel at the Booth." "Oh, sorry you didn't like that one," said Mr. Merrick, "because I *produced* it!" We all had a good laugh over that one.

CARL. I think he plays the dumb card to gain sympathy.

GEORGE. He knows enough to tell Merrick that I'm his assistant.

CARL. Well, Felix likes him. And so does Madame Felix. He'll move up, you wait and see.

GEORGE. That title really bugs you, doesn't it? You really want that.

CARL. I do the best I can. It never seems to be good enough for Felix. And he sets the standards. His is the judgment that we all must seek.

GEORGE. If you think that about NTA, why didn't you get out?

CARL. I'm fifty-one and I've been here twenty-one years. Where would I go? I know what I want. Do you?

GEORGE. I want to be me! Bum rap or halo. Do I have to turn into a nameless, faceless, black-suited piece of jello to make it here? Do I have to live with linoleum leaves on my desk forever?

(He pours scotch in the artificial plant on his desk.)

See? They don't grow and you can't kill them. They're not alive, they're not dead. They just sit there.

CARL. It's only a decoration.

GEORGE. All right, all right.

(pulls off a print from the wall)

So is this skinny old English Virgin a decoration. Do you like her, Carl? I hate her a lot.

CARL. So ignore her. Look out the windows.

GEORGE. Carl, they don't open. Ever. Nobody's windows should be un-openable.

CARL. The air conditioning would be affected.

GEORGE. Screw the air conditioning! But not here. No, take out Wilson, put in Bruin. What's the difference? Same clothes, same prints on the wall, same linoleum leaves, same personalities. Sure, who needs a personality? Check yours in personnel when you enter and Big Brother will give you a new one – company tested, proven efficient, use it free of charge as long as you stay, only don't be disappointed if your own rots away in the check room, cause when you leave it wouldn't fit you any more anyway. By the way, have you noticed? I'm speaking whole sentences, and I'm still standing up.

CARL. You don't need that stuff. Me, I need it – but not you. What the hell – so it didn't work out the way I planned it. But you know, if he gives you the title, and you believe in me, I know I'll make it next time. So give me a chance, huh George? It'll be like a crusade, with you carrying the banners.

GEORGE. Up the rebels!

(He pours.)

You know what I hate? That you had to ask me to help you.

CARL. No, aw –

GEORGE. No, but I will, if I can. If I'm still here. What the hell, we'll beat Brother Bruin at his own nasty game. Let's have another lesson, Carl – I'm getting the hang of this.

(They raise their glasses. There is a knock at the door, and it opens immediately. **LANCE** *rushes in.)*

LANCE. George, Maria is here – what the hell are you doing?

GEORGE. I know you. Now don't tell me –

LANCE. Have you lost your mind? It's eleven o'clock in the morning!

GEORGE. You see Carl how all the wrong people have money?

CARL. *(to* **LANCE:***)* Come in. Come in. Don't just stand there.

GEORGE. I'm studying, Lance. Carl is teaching me how to drink.

LANCE. Yeah, well Maria is ready and she's expecting you.

GEORGE. Tell her I'm too drunk to speak.

LANCE. But I can't sign her without someone's approval.

CARL. I like your zeal. Felix would be proud of you.

LANCE. Felix will never know.

GEORGE. Before you go, let's have a drink to her success.

LANCE. I'm not going – oh, why not?

(He raises his glass. Just then, **HENRY** *walks in.)*

HENRY. What is this? Some kind of a crazy coffee break?

GEORGE. I'm learning how to drink.

(large hiccough)

Let's ask Ellen in for a lesson. She's lousy at it too.

(calls:)

Wolsky!

(He walks out to her. **HENRY** *follows him. Lights up on Secretarial Pool. They are now on in both sections of the set.)*

HENRY. George, it's not Christmas, you know. You can drink alone.

ELLEN. *(looks up from her desk)* Yes, George?

GEORGE. Come on in.

ELLEN. I promised Alec I'd get these out before lunch.

GEORGE. Break it. We're having a drink lesson. With real drinks.

ELLEN. Excuse me. You're having a what?

HENRY. *(to* **GEORGE:***)* Will you calm down? Listen, I took Janet Babcock's headshots to Metro today –

GEORGE. Janet Babcock earns this company forty dollars a year. Do you think this it the time to mention her headshots?

*(***HENRY** *walks* **GEORGE** *back to George's office.)*

MILDRED. *(to* **ELLEN***, when she hears this:)* Honey, you'd better get in there.

ELLEN. I work for them both now. I think the drink lesson can wait till I'm through.

MILDRED. Sweet potato, he sounds a little odd. Like he's plastered.

GLORIA. Is it possible? At eleven o'clock?

GEORGE. Up the rebels!

(He goes to phonograph, puts on a record. It's a pop tune. And loud).

Come on, Henry. If Miss Wolsky won't come in, you dance with me.

MILDRED. *(startled, as she hears music through the open door)* Ellen, get your behind in there!

ELLEN. I have to get these done before Alec gets back.

(She continues typing.)

GLORIA. MiGod, it sounds marvy. I wish they'd invite me.

MILDRED. This isn't happening. All right, you - get in there and turn that thing off.

GLORIA. Well, I don't know. I'm just a girl, and they're four single men.

MILDRED. Now!

*(**GLORIA** enters George's office, and is immediately swept into **GEORGE**'s arms and into a dance. She lets out a whoop, and struggles, but not hard. **LANCE** is dancing by himself. **HENRY.** is watching, amused. **CARL** is suddenly very drunk, and is almost asleep in a chair. Above all this, **MILDRED**'s phone rings. She answers it.)*

MILDRED. Oh my God!

*(She hangs up; she crosses at once to Ellen's desk, and in one quick movement, covers Ellen's typewriter even as **ELLEN** types.)*

Get in there, turn off that record, and send Gloria back. He's on his way down.

ELLEN. Who's on his way down?

MILDRED. Our leader, Felix the First. We've got two minutes!

ELLEN. Mildred, I was writing a letter. That was rude.

MILDRED. If you don't get in there, NOW, close the bar and shut down the disco, there will be no more letters. Understand? There will be un-em-ployment.

ELLEN. You're joking.

MILDRED. This man has no sense of humor. None. Now go, girl, go!

ELLEN. Poor George.

MILDRED. Never mind George. It's the whole damned floor he's after.

(ELLEN runs to GEORGE's office. MILDRED returns to her desk to straighten up.)

MILDRED. Who needs this? My mother was right. I should have been a nun.

ELLEN. *(pulls GLORIA out of GEORGE's arms, somewhat against GLORIA's wishes)* Mr. Fowler's coming down!

(GLORIA lets out a yelp. She pulls free, and runs to MILDRED. The rest happens almost simultaneously)

LANCE. Fowler coming down here?

HENRY. You're joking!

MILDRED. *(to GLORIA)* Clean everything off your desk and throw it in the waste basket.

GLORIA. What?!

MILDRED. I warned you this would happen one day.

GLORIA. You said you'd be tipped off.

MILDRED. I WAS tipped off. Now move!

(MILDRED clears her desk, expertly. She's done it before. In nothing flat, all that remains on it are her phone, her phone-wheel, and one small pad. She moves at once to Ellen's desk to do the same.)

CARL. *(Starts to rise from his stupor)* Felix coming down here? I must greet him. I must meet him at the elevator.

LANCE. Henry, what's to do? He's ossified! I'm half crocked myself. And how do we get George off the dance floor?

HENRY. *(He has turned off the phonograph, but GEORGE continues to dance with ELLEN.)* Take Carl into your office and keep him there until I come for you.

LANCE. Maria Cueva's in there – ready to do a scene.

HENRY. Good. You'll both listen. Now march.

CARL. The elevator, boys. I'll bring him in. Just you wait here.

LANCE. How will I get him into my office? Mildred!

MILDRED. *(from her area)* You're on your own, Junior.

*(They manage to get **CARL** into Lance's office. **HENRY** closes door, moves to George's door, and looks in at him.)*

GLORIA. What'll I do with "Peyton Place?"

MILDRED. In the 'out' basket. He won't look there.

ELLEN. *(dragging **GEORGE** to his desk)* Now you're going to sit very straight, look intelligent, and keep your mouth shut.

GEORGE. You tell Mr. Fowler to make an appointment.

ELLEN. Will you stop wiggling?

GEORGE. No, I will rise!

(He does so, unsteadily.)

ELLEN. *(calling)* Henry, help me!

MILDRED. *(to **HENRY**:)* Stop staring and get in there.

HENRY. Me? I thought I'd take an early lunch.

MILDRED. He needs you!

HENRY. *(on his way into George's office)* How do you do, Mr. Flower? I'm hired. Goodbye, Mr. Fowler. I'm canned. Oh well, I can always go back to dental school.

*(He closes George's door behind him as he enters office. **GEORGE** has collapsed at his desk.)*

Now, what is this nonsense, old timer? The President wants to chat and he thinks enough of you to come down himself to do it.

GEORGE. It's a trap! He thinks I'm asleep.

(His head falls to the desk.)

And I am.

HENRY. You can't let us all down.

GEORGE. *(head still on his arm)* What do I have to do?

HENRY. *(takes his head and lifts it gently)* Well, the first thing is heads up.

GEORGE. Both of them? If you listen, you can hear the whiskey sloshing around.

(He turns his head.)

HENRY. Now listen – in ten seconds Big Brother will be with us. Whatever I say, you agree with me – is that clear?

GEORGE. Of course. But don't discuss politics, religion or sex. What will we discuss?

HENRY. Ellen, get back to your desk.

GEORGE. *(all smiles)* You know Henry, liquor makes my very horny.

ELLEN. Are you sure you can manage alone?

HENRY. I am sure of nothing. Now, get.

(ELLEN returns to her own desk. GLORIA and MILDRED are now at theirs. HENRY sits on George's desk and spreads some of the Beaumont papers. As the lights dim down on George's area, all eyes focus on the Entrance to the Secretarial Pool. – Silence reigns.)

GLORIA. *(after a moment)* Psssst. Mildred.

MILDRED. What is it?

GLORIA. There's coffee on my desk!

MILDRED. Well, get rid of it!

GLORIA. Where, down my dress?

MILDRED. Rosebud, you are bucking for a fat lip.

(GLORIA finally pours it into her artificial leaves. She throws the empty container into the waste basket.)

GLORIA. This whole experience is very degrading.

*(Now **FELIX FOWLER** enters. He's forty-five, and looks younger. He wears all black – tie, socks, suit, shoes, everything visible except a white shirt. He is efficient to the point of making no move without a purpose. There is always calm and quiet in his manner, but one feels the imminence of attack. A coiled cobra is a good image. **ALEC BRUIN** follows right behind.)*

MILDRED. Oh, Mr. Fowler! What a nice surprise.

FELIX. Good morning, Mildred. Ellen. Gloria.

(The SECRETARIES say "good morning," and GLORIA rises.)

GLORIA. Ooooh. Forgive me, Mr. Fowler for speaking, but you know my name!

FELIX. Well, of course I do. And you know mine.

GLORIA. Oh, Mr. Fowler!

ELLEN. Would you like a cookie?

FELIX. What? Oh – yes. You have them here?

ELLEN. Brought them in Monday. They're still fresh.

(She gets the box for him.)

FELIX. Alec, these are worth ten dollars a dozen. I've had them before –

(to ELLEN:)

You really ought to market them.

ELLEN. Aren't you nice?

(offers them to ALEC)

Would you like one? They're oatmeal.

(ALEC takes one.)

ALEC. Thanks.

FELIX. Delicious. Well, I must compliment you all on the way you keep your desks. You know an orderly desk indicates an orderly mind.

MILDRED. We do have a good system.

FELIX. Bright girls. Good girls. Now Ellen. If George is in, I'd like to see him.

ELLEN. Shouldn't I announce you?

FELIX. No need. We're family. Thanks for the cookie.

(He and ALEC walk right into George's office. Lights Down on Pool, up on office.)

HENRY. *(He's peering into George's mouth.)* I think it's swollen, probably infected under the gum. You really shouldn't have come in today.

(He 'notices' the visitors.)

Oh, hello Mr. Fowler. Welcome to New York.

(He moves to shake hands, but **GEORGE** *starts to crumble.* **HENRY** *props him up.)*

Poor George – terrible toothache – upper left bicuspid. I gave him a pill.

ALEC. When did it happen? Ten minutes ago?

HENRY. No, no. Last night.

ALEC. He was fine when I left him.

HENRY. No, no. He was suffering. He just didn't want to put the Beaumont contract aside.

FELIX. Well, get him to a dentist for Pete's sake.

HENRY. I'll take him at lunch.

(He lets **GEORGE** *go for a second, and he starts to fall forward.* **HENRY** *grabs him.)*

I think the medicine hit him hard. George has a very low tolerance.

FELIX. Upper left bicuspid you said. How would you know that?

HENRY. I studied dentistry for two years, Mr. Fowler!

ALEC. Sure you did.

HENRY. The upper left bicuspid has no contact point with the upper left first molar with the result that during mastication, food particles lodge beneath the gingival thus causing breakdown of the fibrous tissues holding the tooth in the socket. So we have the formation of pockets beneath the gingival which have caused a severe state of piarrhea. If the condition is not corrected by an immediate curatage, it could very well become terminal.

(brief pause)

The name's Oldschan, Mr. Fowler. Henry Oldschan – legitimate theatre department.

FELIX. I'm the fellow who hired you. Have you forgotten?

HENRY. Good of YOU to remember, sir. You meet so many people.

ALEC. He looks drunk to me.

*(He pokes at **GEORGE**.)*

HENRY. Don't poke him!

GEORGE. I gave up something too to become an agent.

HENRY. George could have had it made in his father's business – piston rings. But he joined me on the road to real fulfillment with NTA. Right, George?

GEORGE. I am most of the time. Not always, of course.

FELIX. Yes, well – I'll be brief. And then by all means have that attended to. George –

*(**GEORGE** stares at him.)*

Henry, can he hear me?

HENRY. Just say anything that's on your mind. Would you like me to leave, sir?

FELIX. No, I'd like you to stay.

HENRY. Right.

FELIX. We have no secrets here. We have something on our minds, we speak up.

GEORGE. You have something on your mind, YOU speak up.

*(**HENRY** pokes him.)*

FELIX. I want you to know how important this Beaumont problem is. I've just talked to her.

GEORGE. And she doesn't want me?

FELIX. We never got to you. But she's very nervous. She doesn't like to admit it, but if she doesn't do this play, I'm afraid it's back to the ash heap for her.

GEORGE. We've had some very distinguished people in the old ash heap.

FELIX. One must never go back, though. That's worse than never leaving it. Of course not everyone WANTS to leave the ash heap. It has its redeeming features you know.

GEORGE. I can't think of one.

FELIX. Well, for one thing, it's safe. And though it doesn't lead anywhere, it's not very hard to hang on and avoid the garbage man.

GEORGE. That's what's going to happen. The garbage man will get me.

FELIX. How long have you been with us, George?

GEORGE. I was born in 1931.

FELIX. Funny. How long have you been with US?

GEORGE. Oh, us! I know that, too. Six years. Right to the year.

FELIX. And in six years you've learned a lot, I'm sure.

GEORGE. Oh boy – have I learned!

FELIX. Of course you have. NTA is like a master class. It separates the wheat from the chaff, but brother, if that man gets through, he's the best. And George, I don't think you will get through.

GEORGE. Is something going to happen to me?

FELIX. I wanted to find out if you were wheat or chaff.

GEORGE. What's chaff?

FELIX. Worthless matter, refuse.

GEORGE. Henry, I don't feel well.

HENRY. That's the tooth. *(To* **FOWLER***)* And the medicine.

FELIX. It's always exciting, of course – to find out – at last. To know if a man can be a SOMEONE. If he can inherit the mantles of those of us who are getting on.

GEORGE. You mean if you liked my contract, I'd get to replace you?

FELIX. Well, not all at once. But it would have been a start.

GEORGE. Cause I'm not ready to be President. Jeez.

FELIX. No. I'm afraid you're not.

GEORGE. You didn't – like my contract?

FELIX. *(To* **HENRY***)* Did you read it, Henry?

HENRY. No, sir. I did not read it! Not one word.

FELIX. *(To* **ALEC***)* You did, Alec.

(He holds it up, as though it were dirty.)

What did you think of it?

ALEC. Well – the theatre isn't my field.

FELIX. I know that. What did you think of it, anyway?

ALEC. I've seen better.

FELIX. You're hedging.

ALEC. No, it's all right. Except –

FELIX. Ah, of course. Our friend George has disappointed me.

GEORGE. Huh?

FELIX. I'll tell you how.

(Then, to **ALEC***)*

No, you tell him.

ALEC. There's no favored nations clause.

FELIX. That's right. Don't you think that's like a big goof?

ALEC. Well, I told George, in a picture contract, it's essential.

FELIX. And now that Miss Beaumont is cold in California, don't you think leaving it out's going to seem like a slap in her face?

ALEC. Yes, well that's true. She certainly would expect it.

FELIX. You bet your butt she'd expect.

ALEC. So you see, George, it's not a star contract. You forgot the favored nations clause.

GEORGE. *(Just stares at him for a bit. Then as though he'd known it all along)* Oh. Sure. Well, Brother Bruin, I hate to make a liar out of you. But I didn't forget it. I left it out on purpose.

FELIX. Did you hear that? What do you think of that!

ALEC. I don't think you even know what a favored nations clause is because clients like Janet Babcock don't get one.

GEORGE. A favored nations clause, Alec, insures a star that her deal is the very best one in the project, in every detail. It assures her that if any other player is given a contract in which any particular is better than any in her own contract, then her own contract is automatically improved to the point where that situation is remedied.

FELIX. Well, he knows what it is.

(Then to **GEORGE***)*

Then why did you leave it out?

GEORGE. Because it doesn't belong there.

FELIX. I'm not interested in your opinion of its worth. Better minds than yours have fashioned it. The important thing is it's been an integral part of every Beaumont contract since the day we made her powerful enough to demand it.

GEORGE. But it doesn't make any sense in the theatre.

FELIX. Oh, did you hear that, Alec. The theatre?

GEORGE. She's getting ten percent of the gross in this play, and sole star billing, and all the rest that goes with a top star contract. Under no circumstances could Mr. Merrick match that deal with another player, and afford to open the play.

FELIX. Would he have the contractual right to?

GEORGE. I suppose he would, but I just told you – he couldn't possibly do it. Besides, there's no other part in the play for a star.

FELIX. I asked you if he had the right to. That's all.

GEORGE. But this contract is tailored to this actress in this part in this play. Why does it have to conform to a formula? It just isn't done – it's never been done. There are certain traditions. His attorney would think me an amateur – I couldn't even ask for that.

FELIX. I have no intention of having you ask for anything. Alec will ask. Beaumont's coming in tomorrow morning to sign this. You will stay through the meeting because she expects you there and I want nothing to upset her. I told you she was very nervous about doing this play. But if it works it could revive her film career, and she's GOT to do it. So you sit and be quiet and at the proper moment I'll tell her you're not on it any more.

GEORGE. And what happens to me?

FELIX. You go back where you belong, for more seasoning.

GEORGE. Sounds like I'm being roasted on a spit. Oh, you mean the crummy ash heap.

FELIX. You said it. What would be fair? To forgive your error – to permit your sloppiness? To encourage your defiance?

GEORGE. To discuss our differences. Let me convince you you're wrong.

FELIX. There's only one final arbiter in our work. The client. With big clients there can't be even small mistakes. And you made a beaut with Beaumont.

GEORGE. But she won't think so.

FELIX. You've never even met her. I know her, you don't. She will think so. She'll want no part of you.

GEORGE. I've followed her career from day one. She'd be insulted by favored nations. Even if we used it in theatre, it would mean she wasn't important enough to know that no one could match her deal. Can't I talk to her?

FELIX. Can't you see it, Alec? A billion drones yelling "I too have an opinion." No George, no opinions.

GEORGE. But if she's –

FELIX. Forget it. Just get in here at 9:30 tomorrow morning. We'll use your office. I don't want to use the Party Room upstairs. It's too big and formal. I want her to feel cozy and secure. Is that clear?

GEORGE. *(miserable)* Crystal clear.

FELIX. Good. Now get out of here, and have that tooth fixed.

*(He motions for **ALEC** to come with him. They both exit. They pass into the Secretarial Area. Lights On in both areas now.)*

(At this moment, there is a piercing scream from within Lance's office. **FELIX** *and* **ALEC** *stop dead. The* **SECRETARIES** *go on typing, etc. as though nothing were happening. They are used to this. Lance's door flies open, and* **MARIA CUEVA** *stands there, her back to us.)*

MARIA. *(speaking into* **LANCE***'s office)* I've had enough, do you understand? I told you I wanted a child. You promised me I could have a child.

FELIX. Let's get off of this crazy floor!

(He and **ALEC** *exit.)*

LANCE. *(Offstage)* You come back in, I tell you. The neighbors will hear you!

MARIA. I just wanted a baby. And one way or another, I'm going to become a mother.

(She exits, into Lance's office, slams the door.)

MILDRED. *(to the others)* Is there more than one way?

(Lance's door opens, and he sneaks out.)

LANCE. You should hear her. She's great! Carl said I can sign her and she's not even finished yet. He wants her to finish the scene, but I'm going upstairs to get the management papers. Oh, Mildred, I've signed someone There should be trumpets!!

(Exits, DR)

GEORGE. My whole life is passing before me. I see Marvin Marks, my ex-friend who was the first to say to me, "Play it safe."

HENRY. George, calm down.

GEORGE. I am very sick.

HENRY. You've got a head, that's all.

GEORGE. I've got a stomach too. Oh, that was very clever about my teeth.

HENRY. That was nothing. I used to work on corpses.

GEORGE. Used to, hell. You still do.

HENRY. No. The rest of us give the right answers, but you at least wear a red tie once in a while. Only that's not enough.

GEORGE. Once a year I drink, and once a year he comes down to visit. Did they really both happen on the same day!?

HENRY. But boy did you make a start today.

GEORGE. Alec Bruin is still in the Goddamn rowboat!

HENRY. I couldn't have done it. I'd have smiled a lot, and tried to con him. Well, you heard me.

GEORGE. Sure, I fight and you smile a lot. Maybe I should learn to smile.

HENRY. No, tomorrow's just your turn. It's not just you, this whole floor bugs him, oh yes, he's after all of us.

GEORGE. How can I fight? Did you hear the man – "No George, no opinions."

HENRY. Everyone has a part to play. He was playing President.

GEORGE. He was playing God. Wait and see, he's going to prove I'm chaff. Why didn't you hit him, Henry? I mean I couldn't hit him, I couldn't stand up, but you could have punched him right in the mouth.

(He enters his wash room.)

HENRY. You don't punch the President. You'll fight, I don't know how, but if you make it, we all get time off till he smells blood again. If you don't, you start yessing him till he swats you the way he swatted Carl. Or you end up like that idiot Bruin, touching base, kissing ass, writing memos, and standing on your head.

GEORGE. *(returns)* Or I walk out.

HENRY. That's quitting.

GEORGE. What quitting? I wasn't DESTINED to be an agent. It wasn't written in the stars. There are other careers.

HENRY. There are other Felix Fowlers too.

GEORGE. *(He's nauseous)* I'm going home.

HENRY. That's a good idea.

*(**GEORGE** exits to Secretarial Area.)*

ELLEN. *(As he approaches)* Are you all right?

GEORGE. No. I'm all wrong.

ELLEN. Where are you going?

GEORGE. I'm going home. I don't want to kill myself here.

(He exits, DR.)

HENRY. *(following, and exiting too)* Yeah, well afterwards, make a plan for tomorrow!

ELLEN. Mildred, I could just die.

MILDRED. You could make it a double suicide.

(Lance's door flies open again, and MARIA comes out, her back to us.)

MARIA. All right, I'll go. But I won't live out my life alone and lonely. I tell you I'll put an end to it. I warn you Stanley, You will always know you forced me, to take my own life!

(She slams the door, and turns to the LADIES.)

GLORIA. Oooh!

ELLEN. This is not a good day.

MILDRED. *(To MARIA, who needs to know)* Miss Cueva, you're good! It's all right, honey. Just pull up a chair, and join the club.

(CURTAIN)

ACT III

Scene 1

(THE SCENE: George's office. Complete silence.)

*(AT RISE: **FELIX** is seated behind George's desk, facing downstage. When first we see him, it looks as though he might be taking a nap, but we will notice in a moment that he is poring over George's contract, which is in his lap. **ALEC BRUIN** is on the floor, quietly and smoothly doing situps. He looks much as he did in Act II but there has been added a small bandaid over one eyebrow.)*

(TIME: Early the next morning, before 9:30.)

FELIX. God, it's hot. They haven't turned on the air yet.

*(He notices **ALEC** on the floor.)*

Are you still down there? Cut it out, will you Alec?

*(**ALEC** sits in the chair.)*

I didn't sleep at all. Went to bed with two blankets and at two o'clock I thought I was dying. I must have tossed around till half past four before I realized the damned air conditioning was broken. I pushed the cool button and all it did was make noise.

ALEC. I was home early. Must have fallen asleep before the heat hit.

FELIX. Didn't you have a date with Ellen Wolsky?

ALEC. Uh – yes. But I got home early.

FELIX. What's with the bandaid? Did she bite you?

ALEC. No. I scratched myself.

FELIX. Shaving your eyebrows? Well, you probably moved too fast. She's not a Hollywood cutie, you know.

ALEC. I scratched myself this morning. Last night was fine. I got home early, that's all.

FELIX. Just as well. We have a big day and I want to catch the four o'clock flight. Beaumont will fly back with us.

(Puts his handkerchief to the air vent.)

Aha! The building awakens. We'll be able to breathe again.

(Then as though it were the next logical thought.)

What did you think of yesterday?

ALEC. Oh. Well, George does seem to be confused about what's important.

FELIX. Yes. I'll have to un-confuse him.

ALEC. You do know how to do that.

FELIX. It's very hard running both coasts. These New York boys in "the theatre" get sloppy and there's no one here I can trust to run things. Do you think you could get used to the climate?

ALEC. Are you really thinking of me?

FELIX. Henry Oldschan's a good boy but you can sense Wilson's influence over him. He needs a new mentor.

ALEC. I'd love to get my hands on that ninth floor. It needs a watchful eye and a firm hand. Of course, I'd need the authority.

FELIX. Naturally.

ALEC. And if Carol does this play – that would be a starter. You know she likes me. I could keep an eye on Brother Wilson.

FELIX. I don't know, Alec. I haven't made up my mind. My wife would miss you. My daughter would miss you. When she's old enough – who knows? But we need good officers in the field. Those ninth floor agents have more personality than the clients they represent. Which is very very wrong.

ALEC. They all seem more interested in having fun. They kid themselves that the clients are friends. One big happy family. We know what ungrateful rats the clients can be.

FELIX. The fun should come from the work. All we have to be is right, not popular. We have to know. Wilson doesn't understand that without this clause the contract is imperfect, and with a star that just won't do.

ALEC. Well I understand that Felix. And anywhere you think I can be the most helpful, that's where I'll go.

FELIX. I've thought about that.

ALEC. Have you made a decision?

FELIX. No. Relax.

ALEC. Of course. I just want you to know I'm ready.

FELIX. I know you're ready.

(There is a knock on the door.)

That could be George.

ALEC. Do you want me to stay?

FELIX. I want you to stay.

(To the door)

Come in.

(GEORGE *enters. He is wearing a tan summer suit, loafers, and an expensive red tie).*

GEORGE. The door was closed. I hope I'm not interrupting.

FELIX. You're not interrupting .We were waiting for you.

GEORGE. You said nine-thirty.

FELIX. You're not late.

GEORGE. Good. I know this is an important day.

FELIX. How are your teeth?

GEORGE. There was nothing wrong with my teeth. I was drunk.

| **FELIX.** | **ALEC.** |
| You were what? | I told you! |

GEORGE. I had a personal problem, so I drank. Not much. My threshold is very low. But I'm working on that.

FELIX. Your threshold is – ? Well, I'm sorry. Have you come to any conclusions about our talk?

GEORGE. Yes. I have.

FELIX. Good. So have I. During your vast period of research, did it ever occur to you to read one of Beaumont's own contracts? We've done over thirty, I'd say.

GEORGE. They're all picture contracts. They're not relevant.

FELIX. I pride myself on my ability to spot and select the best young men in the country for this company. And then when I think they're ready, I give them a chance. I gave you a chance and you missed the boat.

GEORGE. How? What did I do?

FELIX. *(Flings the contract across the desk at him)* Look at it! It has seven pages of double talk any traffic boy could come up with. You're not dealing with some little ingénue starting life in the sticks. I didn't ask you to come up with a paper for Janet Wilcox who's playing stock in Ohio.

GEORGE. Her name's Babcock.

FELIX. Well that's dandy. But you have to know more than her name – like the difference between a good deal and a bad one. The one you're holding there – that's a bad one. It omits the one thing – the one thing, mind you – that Beaumont will expect, that separates the stock players from the stars, and this you might have discovered for yourself, if you'd spent more time reading her contracts and less time worrying about summer suits which succeed only in making you appear more conspicuous than does your disappointing performance.

GEORGE. Is my suit the problem?

FELIX. It's quite a suit.

GEORGE. I wore it because it's hot today, and it's lightweight.

FELIX. My suit weighs twelve ounces.

GEORGE. I don't like black in summer.

FELIX. Well, well, well. So you're the first one who's had the guts to actually say it. You think I'm the only one who believes in images? What the hell DOES a uniform mean? Order, unity, belonging to something – that's what it means. Big business is run on images – millions are spent to create images. You look intelligent, conservative, sensible, grounded, people believe you are. Confidence gets inspired, clients get signed. But if you showed a breath, just a breath of fresh air, if I saw a little magic in you, if you stood on your own two legs and made a sound, I wouldn't give a damn if you came in in your underwear. How many shares of NTA stock do you own?

GEORGE. What?! Oh. Fifty. I have fifty shares.

FELIX. I have twelve thousand. What do you think that means?

GEORGE. You're VERY rich!

FELIX. It means I am a success. While you –

GEORGE. I know, I know! Well, that's not the only way to tell. I don't mean it isn't nice – Oh God, twelve thousand shares! But that's not the only way to tell. I believe that.

FELIX. I have invested six years in you. In that time, how many clients have you signed?

GEORGE. What? I don't know.

FELIX. How many have we got on Broadway now?

GEORGE. You mean – deals I made?

FELIX. I mean deals you made.

GEORGE. I don't know how many – ten or twelve.

FELIX. How many times a week do you visit them at the theatre?

GEORGE. I don't visit them any times a week. We don't do that.

FELIX. Who's "we"?

GEORGE. "We" is the theatre agents. You visit people on the set in pictures, but we don't do that.

FELIX. Well, maybe that's why you in 'the theatre' are doing so brilliantly.

GEORGE. They'd throw me out if I came to visit. Nobody's allowed backstage after half hour except those connected with the production.

FELIX. When is half hour?

GEORGE. Eight o'clock.

FELIX. What's wrong with before eight o'clock?

GEORGE. Nobody's there! They don't come in until eight o'clock. And if someone does, it's to go over lines, or prepare in some other way, not to talk to agents. We just don't do things the way you do.

FELIX. That has been apparent for some time. Just ask the auditors.

GEORGE. For six years I've heard we don't carry our own weight, that California supports us, but it's not true. I kept a book, and I know it's not true.

FELIX. You kept a what? Did you hear that, Alec? He kept a book.

ALEC. He is colorful.

GEORGE. A black book with blue columns. You get them at Woolworth's. I put down all the commissions my department earns and all the expenses, including rent and travel and insurance and all the things you're going to tell me I left out, and we support ourselves

FELIX. You're not colorful. You're insane.

GEORGE. And what about the performers and writers and all the rest we develop to the point where they become interesting to you out there? Half of them come from my department, from "the theatre" where you can't get in to visit backstage after eight o'clock, and where everybody's not spoiled rotten by agents trying to look necessary by visiting where they're not needed.

FELIX. So you think I'm wrong?

GEORGE. *(Deep breath)* Oh well, why not? Yes. Very wrong. And if this contract displeases you, and it's the first work of mine you've seen since those times two years ago when you screamed at me even worse, then the sum total of my time here must be that you think me a moron. And I am not a moron.

FELIX. Any other complaints?

GEORGE. Is that a loaded question?

FELIX. Feel free.

GEORGE. I think it stinks for you to flay me alive in front of him!

FELIX. Oh, you do?

GEORGE. I cannot answer your questions when you howl at me. I cannot work at all when you howl at me. I am not your prisoner, Mr. Fowler, I am your –

(He cannot think what.)

FELIX. What? Go on. You are my what?

GEORGE. I don't know. Give me a minute. I'll think of something. Colleague?

FELIX. You are my inferior. That's what you are.

GEORGE. And you are a fake! You've been at me forever to stand up and make a sound and now I've made one and you say "forget it" because it's not the sound you'd make. You are a fake, because you don't want me to find – my very own moment and grab it. You want me to sound like you, to dress like you, to BE like you, and I cannot do it. This clause may be nothing by itself – I mean what the hell are we fighting about? – but OK, if you want to fight, we might as well have it out here and now, because I-do-not-believe-in it!

FELIX. *(Starts low, and builds)* Then young man, I suppose it is I who have disappointed you. And I'm deeply sorry about that because I happen to be the President of this company while you have been, and obviously always will be, the rottenest little grey-eyed ash in the ash heap. And if you feel as you do, with all the passion you feel it, then you must write Philip Carey, the Chairman of the Board, and tell him because it sounds like you think you can run this company better than I can!

GEORGE. *(He's losing, and he hates it)* No, I don't – I –

FELIX. That's enough! Not another word, do you hear me?

(The buzzer sounds. He answers the phone.)

Yes. Send her in.

(He gestures to **ALEC.***)*

Alec.

*(***ALEC** *opens the door, and* **CAROL BEAUMONT** *enters. She's vivid, refreshing as an autumn breeze in August. Today she's dressed in something appropriate for Indian Summer in New York. Her age? Probably forty five, maybe more. It's hard to tell.)*

CAROL. Enter Carol Beaumont, to tremendous applause.

FELIX. *(All charm)* Hello, darling.

(She kisses him on the cheek.)

CAROL. Oooh – it's delicious in here. Do you know what's going on outside?

FELIX. It's hard to judge. You look like icy lemonade.

CAROL. At the crack of dawn? You're an agent – through and through.

(She looks around.)

Ah, Alec.

(He moves toward her.)

You know I can't remember seeing you in long pants. Turn around.

(He does, awkwardly.)

Hmmm – pretty. But you're even prettier when you're OUT of uniform.

(She turns to **GEORGE.***)*

And you must be George Wilson.

GEORGE. How do you do, Miss Beaumont?

CAROL. How do you do?

(She offers her hand.)

Oh Felix – he's nice.

(then, to **GEORGE***)*

How does it feel to be the fair haired boy?

GEORGE. I beg your pardon?

CAROL. I've been with NTA for twenty years. I'm family. I know when big things are brewing for one of the boys. It's very pleasant meeting you at last.

GEORGE. *(Looks at* **FELIX***, who give him no encouragement)* Well, thank you.

CAROL. *(Turns back to* **FELIX***)* So – now that we're all friends, where's the coffee? Felix, you can't expect me to get up before breakfast and not give me coffee.

FELIX. Of course. Alec, ask Marcel to fix us a tray.

*(***ALEC** *goes off to do so.)*

CAROL. Really, have you ever seen such weather? It's very tough on us ladies I can tell you – the war paint just r-un-s. Are my eyes on, Felix? I wouldn't want to disgrace you.

FELIX. You could face a close up in Cinemascope.

CAROL. Sweet. Are you a native New Yorker, Mr. Wilson?

GEORGE. No. I emigrated from Bayonne.

CAROL. You're the REALLY devoted kind, then. Like me. God, I'd forgotten the park and the energy and the marvelous shops – all the places I couldn't afford when I lived here. Well I'm going back today and g-or-ge myself. Heat or no heat.

GEORGE. Uh – no more two hour splurges at Woolworth's?

CAROL. No more what?

GEORGE. I guess you've forgotten.

CAROL. Well, remind me.

GEORGE. I once read an interview in which you said you'd throw quarters in a bottle for months and then you'd take them to Woolworth's and spend two hours buying out the store.

CAROL. I'VE forgotten? Why no. But that interview was printed in nineteen ought four. How in the world do YOU remember?

GEORGE. I guess it impressed me.

CAROL. Well my dear boy, I still DO that. Felix, do you know what you can buy at Woolworth's? I think if I hadn't landed in show business I'd have been a very happy bookkeeper. Do you know I STILL do my own income tax? I write everything down and although my marvelous Manny White keeps me out of jail, I keep the records. And all with supplies from Woolworth's. They have ten cent pencil sharpeners that are much better than those fancy electric things, and ball point pens that never run dry and self-seal envelopes that Cartier's can't copy. And those marvelous black books with blue columns. Have you ever seen one of them?

FELIX. Yes, well I'm sure Woolworth's has its place in the scheme of things. But it's time –

CAROL. Has its place! Have you ever tried one of their carrot peelers? Hoffritz be damned, they're fifteen cents and there's just no other way to peel a carrot.

GEORGE. I'm very big for their picture hooks myself.

CAROL. The new kind – that you don't nail in, you just lick!

GEORGE. That's right. No more holes in the wall.

CAROL. And the marvelous thing is I don't feel I'm paying for anything. It's always those quarters. When I was a kid it was pennies and I used a pickle jar for a bank. Now it's quarters and a great glass thing from Steubens. From pickle jar to Steubens, but a Woolworth Girl all the way. And thank you Mr. Wilson for reminding me of it all.

GEORGE. Call me George.

(Trying to stay alive.)

You know what I do? I have two bank accounts.

CAROL. No! I have six. Isn't it marvelous?

GEORGE. One of mine is for putting in, one is for taking out.

CAROL. I INVENTED that system. Who told you about it?

GEORGE. I thought I made it up.

CAROL. But I do that too! Felix, when I was an understudy I had two bank accounts. There was eleven dollars in one and six in the other, but I felt so secure.

(The door opens, and ALEC re-enters with a tray of coffee.)

Oh thank God – the coffee man.

ALEC. You take it black, don't you Carol?

(She blows a kiss, "Yes.")

FELIX. Boys, help yourselves.

(They do, during the next speeches.)

CAROL. *(to FELIX)* I feel very important, darling. When I used to visit Carl Murray downstairs, I'd have to SNEAK coffee in in my handbag. I'm delighted at last you feel I'm housebroken.

(ALEC hands her a cup.)

Thank you.

(To GEORGE)

Tell me more about you, George. How did you get to be Felix's east coast favorite?

FELIX. Carol, we don't want to take your whole morning. You've got shopping and we have a plane to catch. Don't you think we should address ourselves to the contract?

CAROL. Oh dear, I knew the moment would come. Now Felix, you must listen to me. And I don't mean tolerantly, like you did yesterday. Felix, I cannot, and I mean can-not do this play.

(She lets that sink in for a moment.)

I know my last three films did not earn back their negative costs and I know that means I am down the drain in lotus land. But darling, I'm not exactly broke, I have a husband who loves me, and I'm confident that if no one will have me for hire then I can just bloody well buy myself a story, develop it, and set up a production all by my lonesome.

FELIX. And who will finance you? Your husband?

CAROL. No. One of the many reasons we're good together is that Charles said right up front: "Me no invest in show business." Oh darling, you're so marvelous with money things – I'll buy the property. YOU get it financed.

FELIX. Sure. Well it won't work. The time to set up your own package is the week AFTER you break the record at the Music Hall. Not after three mistakes.

CAROL. And what about my eleven record breakers with combined grosses of seventy MILLION dollars? What's that my dear Felix, bologna and eggs?

FELIX. You like this play, and this part – you've admitted that.

ALEC. And Carol, if I can put in my two cents, you're one of the few film gals who isn't going to make a fool of herself on stage. You know your way around the footlights like a cat around an alley.

CAROL. What a sweet thought.

(Then to **FELIX***)*

Fifteen years is a long time, Felix. It's not like riding a bike. You forget.

FELIX. Don't your awards mean anything? Just take them out and look at them once in a while.

CAROL. I'd have to sandblast the dust off them. And they were for movies, where I got a lot of help from cinematographers and composers writing music to make me sound like I knew what I was doing. Onstage, you're on your own, like an acrobat without a net.

FELIX. Carol, we've been through all this. This decision is yours. But I will not sit back and see you taking second best in Hollywood.

CAROL. Who's talking second best? We'll make our own movie – something marvelously arty that will win all the prizes in Venice. Oh come on Felix, where's your fighting spirit? Remember how you fought to get me "Promise of Winter"? You told me you knew I'd get the Oscar before we shot one frame of that picture. What's happened to that marvelous kind of blind faith? I'm still the same girl.

FELIX. We were younger then.

CAROL. What can I do about that?

FELIX. You can do this play.

CAROL. Felix, if you don't think you can find me a story and a set-up, then I'll have to find me an agent who can. And don't think your brothers in black haven't done everything but pitch tents in my garden. Because they have.

FELIX. I'm sure you'll find them under every rock. And what do they offer you? Percentage deals, profit sharing deals except there's never any profit on the books? Capital gains? Crap. That's agent talk, and it runs fast and loose in the mating season. Ask me how I know? I know. I invented nine-tenths of it.

CAROL. You're certainly not using any of it now.

FELIX. I care what happens to you.

CAROL. Why? I'm just a name on a list. Scratch me off, you lose a quarter of an inch. It will still be the biggest list on both coasts.

FELIX. This from you? From the girl who publicly thanked me when she won her Oscar?

CAROL. As you said – we were younger then.

FELIX. All right. Can the sentiment. It doesn't belong here anyway. Let's say I care because I've got a twenty year investment in you. And I'll be damned if I'll turn you loose for someone else to cash in on it.

CAROL. Cash in on what? I thought you said there was a "No Sale" sign on Beaumont.

FELIX. Oh no, there's a lot of mileage left in you.

CAROL. You make me sound like a racehorse.

FELIX. I mean it. There's third parts in big pictures, summer stock, a "cameo role" in an epic, Broadway in a bad play, a long tour in a good one. I'd say three years. THEN you'll leave your new agents and come back to us. And they will have cleaned up, only you My Dear Beaumont will be out of business.

CAROL. You paint a vivid picture.

FELIX. I don't believe in lies.

CAROL. You don't believe in anything my darling. I think I'll just sit on my hilltop, look at my Oscar, keep house for my husband, and wait for "Son of Sunset Boulevard" to come along.

FELIX. That's quitting, damnit! What the hell's happened to you?

CAROL. Remember, I'm not as young as I – You go play eight shows a week in front of eleven hundred killers.

FELIX. Is there anything I can say to convince you I'm right?

CAROL. Sorry darling, I guess for the first time in all our years together, I believe in me more than you do.

FELIX. Well, it's not that simple. We made a deal for you, with your approval. The press has carried it, Merrick's booked theatres, a staff has been assembled, parties have been arranged.

CAROL. Well, un-arrange them. You're a genius at that.

FELIX. I don't want to un-arrange them. I'm not helping you commit suicide.

CAROL. Now stop it, Felix. You're not the dramatic type.

FELIX. I mean it. You've always listened to me on career choices. I know what's right for you.

CAROL. Maybe you once did. I don't like learning we're not on the same page any more than you do.

FELIX. But we are.

CAROL. No. People change. You don't know me any more.

FELIX. I warn you they'll tell the truth and I can't stop them. Merrick won't let you just fade away. There'll be no press release about your 'other commitments.' There are no other commitments. He'll say you walked out, that you were scared, and there's nothing I can do to stop him.

CAROL. You mean there's nothing that you will do. So I'm back where I began – on my own.

FELIX. No. You'll do this play. You will!

CAROL. Sorry darling, I'm not in your employ. You seem to have forgotten that you work for me.

(She starts to leave.)

GEORGE. Miss Beaumont, do you remember the last performance you gave in "Imitation"?

CAROL. *(She is stumped for a moment)* As a matter of fact, I do.

GEORGE. And that was the last time you appeared on a stage?

CAROL. I guess it was.

GEORGE. Do you remember your final curtain call?

CAROL. *(Another beat, while she recalls)* Oh Felix, that was SUCH a night. John Golden, the producer, made a speech all about me. I mean the play was going to run on without me, but my year's contract was up and I was going to Hollywood so he made a special fuss. And then he asked me to say something and the whole audience threw confetti at me – and I started to cry and I couldn't stop. And then the audience – I could hear them – I could feel them crying with me. If anyone had wandered in, they'd have thought we were out of our minds. Eleven hundred people all saying goodbye to me.

GEORGE. Eleven hundred killers I think you called them.

CAROL. What? Oh. Well silly, that was my closing night. Closing nights are very special, Everybody cries.

GEORGE. Did you ever stop crying and make your speech?

CAROL. Oh yes, I made my speech and then they all cheered and threw more confetti.

GEORGE. What did you say?

CAROL. I thanked them for their tears and for their applause. I really felt very close to them that night I suppose. And then I told them I had a one-picture deal and that whether they liked it or not, I'd be back as soon as the picture was finished.

GEORGE. And then they cheered?

CAROL. And then they cheered.

GEORGE. Well, Miss Beaumont, that picture's been finished a long time.

CAROL. Oh come, Mr. Wilson – that was fifteen years ago. Nobody believed me. Closing nights are always sloppy and sentimental.

GEORGE. I believed you.

CAROL. You were there?!

GEORGE. In my usual perch. Last row of the balcony.

CAROL. You must have been twelve.

GEORGE. I was sixteen. I threw more confetti than anyone.

CAROL. I've always wondered. Where did you all get it?

GEORGE. The ushers gave it to us in the intermission.

CAROL. They were in on it too?

GEORGE. Everybody said goodbye to you. And everybody cried because you really did have something for us, and you were taking it away.

CAROL. Felix, take HIM away. He's from another era. Are you suggesting, Mr. Wilson, I've let my public down?

GEORGE. For a long time I felt you'd let ME down. But as you say, fifteen years is a long time, and even sentimental young men in the balcony grow up. But haven't you missed what happened that night?

CAROL. Of course I've missed it. Do you KNOW the waves of love that roll in from an audience?

GEORGE. Well, isn't that still waiting for you?

CAROL. How do you know?

GEORGE. How do we know anything? We know.

CAROL. It doesn't just happen. You have to earn it – all over again.

GEORGE. A minute ago you said you believed in yourself more than – we did.

CAROL. Look dear, I know what coming back is like. They wait for you. I'm a film lady now, and we are sitting ducks. Oh no young man, I could be tarred and feathered.

GEORGE. You could also be exalted.

CAROL. I've seen my sisters of the silver screen come limping back to California after two glorious weeks on the main stem. Some of them never recover.

GEORGE. They didn't have this play, this part, this producer. They didn't have your experience, or your talent. They didn't have us behind them, believing in them.

CAROL. Well, they didn't have YOU, that's for sure.

GEORGE. Don't be scared, Miss. Beaumont. You don't really want to make arty movies, you want to do this play. You're scared because you're a big talent, and big talents all get scared. Anybody can come out and say the words and never bat an eyelash, but you don't do things that way, you never have. You've got a hell of a job ahead of you, but you've got the stuff. You've proved that.

CAROL. George, you're sweet. But you're very young.

GEORGE. I've been at NTA for six years. Young I'm not. And we all know the responsibility we're assuming in urging you to do this. We just accept it because we're certain we're right.

CAROL. You do make it sound simple. Of course it wouldn't be simple.

GEORGE. But then what worth having ever is?

CAROL. Well – perhaps if I thought about it a little –

GEORGE. Do you KNOW what Woolworth's is like at Christmas? They really swing at Christmas!

CAROL. You're romanticizing again. It's refreshing as hell, and I'm a sucker for it, but Woolworth's at Christmas is a very silly symbol and has nothing to do with the reaction to me in a play.

ALEC. Yes, what's Woolworth's got to do with –

FELIX. Alec, shut up.

GEORGE. It's a symbol, but it's also a good start. Put yourself in my romantic little picture and see if the juices don't begin to flow. And once that happens and all those people behind you start to push, well come on Miss Beaumont, where's your sense of adventure? Have you lost it? Are you saying no because you're scared? That's no reason, not for you. You made a promise and you have to keep it. You owe it to yourself, to that audience. You even owe it – to me.

CAROL. I've had this conversation before – with myself. All right, I'm scared. God knows I never thought I'd say it and why I'm telling you, some total stranger, I'll never know. But you do seem to understand, so I'll admit – it's just easier my way. We only have so many knock-down, drag-outs in us, and I just don't want to fight no more.

(She laughs, suddenly.)

Oh don't worry, I'm not insane. I just remembered, years ago, I played "A Month In The Country" in stock – that's quite a play to do in one week, try it sometime – and Natalia Petrovna, whose lover and best friend both desert her at the same time, leaving her with a husband she doesn't love, looks back before her final exit and says –

GEORGE. "You're the salt of the earth. You're both the salt of the earth. And yet – and yet –."

CAROL. Exactly. Will someone tell me why I thought of that?

GEORGE. Do you want to end up like her, drying up in a desert, frustrated and empty?

CAROL. No, I do not. All right. Give me the pen and let me make my mark. Quickly, quickly. God help me, I'm coming back to Broadway.

(**GEORGE** *gives her a pen.*)

Is it all right, Felix? Am I protected from all the terrible things that can happen?

ALEC. What about the favored nations clause?

FELIX. We can send that to you as a rider after Mr. Merrick initials it.

CAROL. What favored nations clause? Don't be silly.

ALEC. Carol, you've always had it. Don't you be silly.

CAROL. Second raters might need favored nations in the theatre. Do you still think I need it?

ALEC. Felix, didn't you say –?

FELIX. I say, "Alec you're out of your league." I say let's sign the contracts.

CAROL. *(As she signs)* Darling, this is a play. Mr. Wilson, this is your contract. Didn't you tell him about plays?

GEORGE. Well, I –

CAROL. Of course you did. We don't need favored nations with plays. I guess that's why it's called the "legitimate theatre."

(*She finishes signing, and hands the contracts to* **FELIX**.)

Here you are darling. My last will and testament. I just hope it isn't a lingering death.

FELIX. Well, I'm very pleased. This is a big moment.

GEORGE. There ought to be champagne.

CAROL. There ought to be a doctor and men in white coats.

ALEC. Felix, don't you think Carol should reconsider about that clause?

CAROL. Alec, go stand on your head. You know the last time I signed one of these, Carl Murray sneaked me a double scotch. Where is Carl? Do you think he'd mind my dropping in unannounced?

GEORGE. He'd love that.

CAROL. Well, I must see him. He pushed me through my early years – you pulled me through the middle, Felix – and now George is going to carry me through old age. God bless us all.

GEORGE. Would you like me to take you down to Carl's office?

CAROL. I know my way. Thanks. Goodbye, George – for a while. I'll be back in a month, and we'll talk. I want you to know all about me before we ride the last mile together.

GEORGE. I'll look forward to it.

(She is at the door now. As an afterthought, she turns.)

Oh Alec, darling – do you ice skate?

ALEC. Ice skate? No, I don't. Not much call in California.

CAROL. Yes dear, well do learn. If Beaumont is going to spend the winter trying to please the carriage trade, with only occasional visits from her husband, she's going to have to do something on Sundays, and I find ice skating relaxing and marvelous exercise. Felix, you will let Alec come east once in a while, won't you?

FELIX. We'll see.

CAROL. What am I saying? We'll probably close in Boston, on the way in.

GEORGE. NTA girls never close in Boston.

CAROL. Philadelphia? *(She laughs)* Oh Felix, you were absolutely right as always. He's divine! You must give him an enormous raise.

(She exits. There is a pause. Long.)

GEORGE. Well, I mean there we were at loggerheads, and I certainly don't expect that just because Carol Beaumont agreed to do this play –

FELIX. How did you do it?!

GEORGE. She said she was a film lady. But she's not really. She's theatre. I guess I am too.

ALEC. Yes, I've often found with real film people, they just –

GEORGE. And I must say – Felix – I wouldn't accept a raise even if you offered me one. What I really want to know is, whether you think I have a chance of – rising from those ashes.

FELIX. Why you little bastard. That's line for line from my book!

GEORGE. It is?

FELIX. I wrote a book. And you just lifted a whole paragraph.

GEORGE. I did? You know, that's happened before. It must be part of my subconscious.

FELIX. "If you want a raise, be sure not to ask for it. Just ask about your future. The boss will force you to accept more money because he'll be convinced you've been offered a better job elsewhere."

GEORGE. Of course it's from your book! Oh I could die of embarrassment. But when you write a classic, I guess you have to expect to be quoted.

FELIX. You're the first east coast man who's ever read it. I didn't think you guys had even heard of it.

GEORGE. Heard of it! Why your chapter on being indispensable has chartered my career. Alec and I were discussing it yesterday, weren't we Alec? Isn't that funny?

ALEC. We weren't discussing it – I was –

FELIX. Well, I'll fool you. I've got something better than a raise. But let me sleep on it.

GEORGE. Oh, sure. Well sir, I've got to wash up for lunch. And then, could I please have my office back?

(He moves to bathroom door.)

Oh Alec – if you need any assistance in collecting your things, before you leave, just let me know, and I'll find someone – to assist you. Ciao!

(He exits into the bathroom.)

ALEC. He wore that tan suit and he defied you, didn't he?

FELIX. Did you see him? Oh Alec, I was right about him all the time. And he's read my book.

ALEC. Yeah, well when do you suppose he did that?

FELIX. If he had any of me in him, he'd have read it for the first time last night. Of course that's asking a lot. What do you think?

ALEC. What do I think? You don't want to know.

FELIX. Watch him, Alec. You can learn from him.

ALEC. Why do you favor him like that? You never let me get out of line.

FELIX. I didn't let him do anything. He took his moment. He took it! You could have done that a hundred times.

(Through the above speech, **FELIX** *has moved to the door, taking the contracts with him.)*

ALEC. And what about my crack at the title? Is that one of the things you're going to sleep on?

FELIX. No. I've already slept on that.

(He goes out. **ALEC** *moves toward bathroom to have final words with George, stops, reconsiders. Then, slowly, he too exits.)*

(CURTAIN)

Scene 2

(SETTING: The Secretarial Area again.)

*(AT RISE: **MILDRED** is onstage, on phone. **GEORGE** is in his office, behind his desk. But no light there, so we can't see him.)*

(TIME: Ten minutes later.)

MILDRED. That's right, Mrs. Miller, three coffees. Today?

*(**HENRY** enters from DR. He's dressed in the usual, but today he's sporting a vivid yellow tie.)*

HENRY. *(crossing to his office)* Good morning, Mildred. Is George through with his meeting?

MILDRED. I haven't seen him.

HENRY. Let me know, will you?

MILDRED. *(She notices **HENRY**'s yellow tie)* Henry!

(He turns at his door, lets us really see it. Maybe He touches it. He smiles at her, and shrugs. The shrug says "It's a beginning anyway." He exits into his office.)

*(**ELLEN** comes out of **LANCE**'s office.)*

ELLEN. Have you heard from George?

MILDRED. Now, doll. It's just ten o'clock.

ELLEN. I've been looking out the window. At least he hasn't left the building.

MILDRED. Did you expect him to sail past?

ELLEN. No. I'm sure he'll have great success.

MILDRED. That's more like it.

ELLEN. Mildred, I didn't sleep last night.

MILDRED. Why? Wasn't it fun with Alec the Rat?

ELLEN. No, I was home early. We took a walk and sat awhile and then he groped me.

MILDRED. Oh, I want him for my charm bracelet.

ELLEN. He's just awful. Everything George said about him was true.

MILDRED. As opposed to what I said about him.

ELLEN. And when I didn't sleep I went over it all again. Actually, I thought it was cute how George got sick in the Men's Room at Bloomingdale's. It was my mother, you see.

MILDRED. She got sick in the Men's Room too?

ELLEN. My mother and her damned articles. "You should this, you shouldn't that."

MILDRED. You'd better write this down. You're going to forget this.

ELLEN. I love George because he wants to be more than he is. I mean no two roses are exactly alike. Why should any two people be?

MILDRED. Now that you ask, I can't imagine.

ELLEN. You don't throw a rose in the garbage – unless it's rotten.

MILDRED. I've met some pretty rotten roses.

ELLEN. I've always been afraid to take chances. Let's be honest, I'm "Miss Careful." But now I find it exciting just to think about going along with George wherever he's going. I like to be led. I'm a nurturer. That's who I am.

MILDRED. *(to the air)* Graduation day. She finally figured it out.

(The buzzer rings twice, on Ellen's desk.)

ELLEN. Oh my God, he's in his office! Mildred, really – what should I do?

MILDRED. Sharpen his pencils, sit on his lap, and say yes to everything.

*(**ELLEN** runs off into George's office. Lights Up on his office area.)*

ELLEN. How long have you been here? Are you all right?
GEORGE. I'm fine. Ellen, sit down.
ELLEN. I didn't bring my pad. Do you want to dictate?
GEORGE. No.
ELLEN. How did your meeting go?

GEORGE. I think I'm getting a raise. Maybe more.

ELLEN. Oh. Then you didn't get fired?

GEORGE. No. Ellen, I had a rotten day yesterday.

ELLEN. You too?

GEORGE. I went right home from here, and I thought a lot about what you said.

ELLEN. You really should not have listened. I've been very upset lately.

GEORGE. No, you were right. You've always been there whenever I needed you. And it can't have been much fun for you.

ELLEN. Well –

GEORGE. Yesterday I was all keyed up about Fowler and Beaumont and Bruin. I wandered around the apartment like a wild man thinking very hard, and when I was through I had a very big shock.

ELLEN. What do you mean?

GEORGE. There was no one to talk to about it. And I didn't want Lance or Henry or Mildred. I wanted you.

ELLEN. Well, you could have called me.

GEORGE. I didn't think I had the right.

ELLEN. Why not? I *am* your secretary.

GEORGE. I didn't want my secretary. I wanted – you. That's where the shock came in.

ELLEN. Yes, that is a shock.

GEORGE. You see, when something good finally happened to me, I wanted to share it with you. Ellen, I don't want to be a loner any more.

ELLEN. So?

GEORGE. Don't you think that's a big step forward?

ELLEN. Oh yes, That's big. That's big!

GEORGE. So what do you say?

ELLEN. To – to what? Well – whatever what – I – I say – yes!

GEORGE. Good. Now you should know that some of what you told me I can't use. Like if I tell you we're flying to London for the weekend, you'll pack our bags and get ready, right?

ELLEN. London? Pack our bags, right.

GEORGE. Good. Because fear won't be of any use to us. Now of course if you don't like how I treat you – ever – you'll tell me right to my face. Like yesterday, right?

ELLEN. Yes. And of course you'll tell me too.

GEORGE. Oh, absolutely. That way we should have a very good life together. So. Well –

(He rises and comes from behind his desk. He comes at her, differently than ever before.)

ELLEN. Oh dear. Oh George. Darling George. Oh yes. Wow! Oh dear.

(She moves toward him, and they kiss. During the next, till her exit, they kiss a lot, even with the door open.)

GEORGE. So can we start with lunch?

ELLEN. Any time.

GEORGE. Shall I pick you up at one?

ELLEN. Pick me up? I'm next door.

GEORGE. Still…

ELLEN. Fine. By all means, pick me up. Now I must go. My boss is a terrible tyrant.

GEORGE. But they say once you get to know him – .

ELLEN. Yes. Oh yes.

*(She exits, and closes the door. As she moves DR, she notices the pile of articles on her desk, and gracefully dumps them in the wastebasket, which has been pre-set below her desk. She embraces **MILDRED**, who is agog at all the kissing in the doorway.)*

MILDRED. I don't know what you think I told you, but whatever it is, tell ME!

*(They exit together, Down R. **GEORGE**, happy, finds his plaque, picks it up, He wonders if he dares, and decides to hang it. HE tries one spot, moves it higher up the wall. As he's adjusting it, the door opens suddenly, and **FELIX***

is standing there, holding the Beaumont contracts. **ALEC** *is behind him.)*

FELIX. George!

GEORGE. *(A beat. Steps down from the sofa. Calmly)* Mr. Fowler.

FELIX. I should have left these here. Let's go over them together. Come see me after lunch.

(He hands him the contracts. He goes to the door, then turns back. He looks at the plaque.)

George, I'd like it a lot better – if you hung it a little lower?

GEORGE. Hm? Oh. Yes. Thanks!

FELIX. *(to* **ALEC***)* Coming ?

ALEC. In a minute. I've got to get my things.

*(***FELIX** *exits.* **GEORGE** *disappears behind his desk, gets out the scotch, pours a drink.)*

I have to get my golf shoes.

GEORGE. Help yourself.

ALEC. *(During this, he gets the shoes from desk drawer)* And I wanted to congratulate you. Felix was very impressed. I was too! We were both off the mark on this one. I have to admit it, I've always been a sort of bottom line sort of guy – I'm not much into psychology. But you, George – you make an effort to understand people, to know how to manipulate them, to know which levers to pull. Yes sir, I'll bet I could learn a trick or two from you. I mean, we're both #1 in Felix's eyes , but the sands shift if you know what I mean and we should look out for each other. I'm sure that if we work together, we can get Carol through this major career move of hers. So when I come back this winter, how about it? No hard feelings?

(He offers his hand.)

GEORGE. *(He shakes his hand)* Oh, no! No hard feelings. I was just about to toast Janet Babcock – you know, her making it to the wall and all. Would you like to join me?

(He offers him a drink.)

ALEC. I knew you'd understand, George. I mean I can read people too. And I'm glad. I know we're going to work well together from now on.

GEORGE. So. "Fortuna vobiscum saecula saeculorum."

ALEC. I know, I know. *(a beat)* What does it mean?

GEORGE. Oh, right, you don't dig latin. Well, when I say it to Janet it means "May luck be with you forever and ever."

ALEC. Nice. That's nice.

GEORGE. But when I say it to you, it sort of means –

(He raises his thumb to his nose, and emits a loud raspberry.)

*(**ALEC** just stares. **GEORGE** swallows the scotch, makes a face. He is stuck with his high ideals and his low tolerance for whiskey.)*

(THE CURTAIN IS DOWN.)

PROPERTY PLOT

ACT I SCENE 1
1. All desk telephones (3 in Secretarial Pool, 2 on George's desk) with push buttons for one or two lines, and a buzzer button to ring from secretary to boss.
2. A framed plaque (at least 8"x10") that is hangable on a wall, should read: "Most Promising Actress. 1962-63 JANET BABCOCK as "Linda Seton" in "Holiday".
3. 3 containers of coffee in a brown bag, or store bag.
4. 1 Astrology handbook for Gloria.
5. Steno pads for 3 secretaries.
6. 1 box of homemade cookies for Ellen to bring in.
7. 2 suitcases for George for his entrance.
8. 1 cup and saucer for Ellen's closet.
9. A pile of phone message sheets.
10. Janet Babcock's newspaper reviews (at least three of them)
11. Interoffice memo from Alec Bruin for Henry Oldschan's entrance.
12. Memos, mail for Ellen to show George.
13. Bottle or tin of antacid pills for George's desk.
14. Phi Beta Kappa key (or similar) for George's tie

ACT I SCENE 2
Phonograph and recording of female vocalist

8"x10" photos for Henry to thumb through

$20 cash for Henry to give LANCE. Scotch bottle and glass in George's desk drawer

Small suitcase (gym bag) for Alec Bruin

A pair of golf shoes Alec's gym bag.

ACT II
A pile of contracts (2 or 3 copies) for George at top of act.

Articles – news clippings on Ellen's desk.

4 more glasses in George's desk for Scotch drinks.

LP records for phono for 'drinking scene'

"Peyton Place" book for Gloria's desk

Coffee in a cardboard cup on Gloria's desk

ACT III
A tray of coffee and cups in china, spoons, for Alec to bring in for CAROL. A pen for George to give Carol, for signing contracts.

THE WHOLE NINTH FLOOR

**Also by
Richard Seff...**

Paris Is Out!

**Shine!:
The Horatio Alger Musical**

Please visit our website **samuelfrench.com** for complete descriptions and licensing information

From the Reviews of
THE WHOLE NINTH FLOOR...

"...A moment's concentration brings home...the basic fact that Seff weaves a story based on the young man's intense and insistent desire to do the right thing. The laughs come fast, and they are plentiful."
- Kenneth G. Wallace, *The Patterson Call*

"The funniest scene drives him to down a few drinks...What ensues is a masterpiece. This play can develop into a brilliant work. Producer Robert Ludlum appears to have another hit."
- *The Sunday Post*

"The comedy construction of *The Whole Ninth Floor* is made up of wall-to-wall witticisms. Seff has a good ear and facile pen for manufacturing witty dialog. He obviously knows–from first hand experience—Madison Avenue and the talent agency area of show business, for his prototypes and inside trade references are accurate and appropriate."
- *The Scotch Plain Times*

"A sparkling new comedy, a tremendously funny play, with a second act wild drinking part that is its highlight."
- Tom Vaughan, *The Herald News*

OTHER TITLES AVAILABLE FROM SAMUEL FRENCH

JACK GOES BOATING
Bob Glaudini

Full Length / Comedy / 2m, 2f / Interior

Four flawed but likeable lower-middle-class New Yorkers interact in a touching and warmhearted play about learning how to stay afloat in the deep water of day-to-day living. Laced with cooking classes, swimming lessons and a smorgasbord of illegal drugs, *Jack Goes Boating* is a story of date panic, marital meltdown, betrayal, and the prevailing grace of the human spirit.

"An immensely likable play [that] exudes a wry compassion."
- *The New York Times*

"Endearing romantic comedy about a married couple and the social-misfit friends they fix up. Witty and knowing and all heart."
- *Variety*

"Glides effortlessly from the shallow end of the emotional pool to the deep end."
- *Theatremania.com*

SAMUELFRENCH.COM